Fixing

Flamingos

AND OTHER SOLUTIONS TO THE WORLD'S LEAST PRESSING PROBLEMS

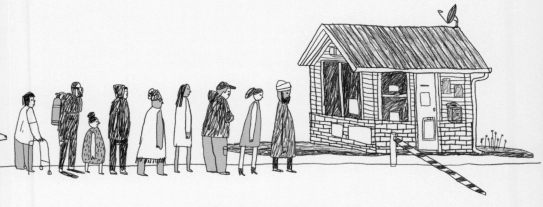

Brian Rea

Lucienne Brown

CHRONICLE BOOKS
SAN FRANCISCO

Library of Congress Cataloging-in-Publication Data:
Names: Rea, Brian, author. | Brown, Lucienne, author.
Title: Fixing flamingos : and other solutions to the world's least pressing
problems / Brian Rea, Lucienne Brown.
Description: San Francisco : Chronicle Books, 2023.
Identifiers: LCCN 2023005657 | ISBN 9781797218755 (paperback)
Subjects: LCGFT: Experimental fiction. | Humorous fiction.
Classification: LCC PS3618.E2125 F59 2023 | DDC 811.6—dc23/eng/20230217
LC record available at https://lccn.loc.gov/2023005657

Manufactured in China.

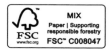

Design by Allison Weiner.
Typesetting by Maureen Forys and Ashley McKevitt
of Happenstance Type-O-Rama.

10 9 8 7 6 5 4 3 2 1

Chronicle books and gifts are available at special quantity discounts to
corporations, professional associations, literacy programs, and other organizations.
For details and discount information, please contact our premiums department
at corporatesales@chroniclebooks.com or at 1-800-759-0190.

Chronicle Books LLC
680 Second Street
San Francisco, California 94107
www.chroniclebooks.com

To Rudy, Frankie, Thea, Raffy and Moon.

Thanks to Natalie, Allison, and the team—you have been a joy
to work with. Brian, I am so grateful for your generosity of spirit,
kindness, and support. Here's to many more years of laughter and
questionable hairstyles.
—LB

For Miko, Luka, and K.

Special thanks to Natalie Butterfield, Allison Weiner, and the rest
of the Chronicle team who brought this book to life; to Lucie, for
your light and laughter and willingness to collaborate throughout
the pandemic; and to all the Abbys in the world who read this
book, see the world in a new way, and dedicate themselves to
fixing things down there.
—BR

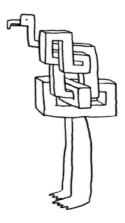

FIXING FLAMINGOS

My name is Abby.

I am an intern in what you probably know as Heaven, but we now call Up Here. We rebranded recently to appeal to the nonreligious, but it's probably just as you imagine: crystal staircase, pearly gates, fluffy clouds, the whole shebang (but with a few surprises). The new logo is pretty cool—I'll show you when it's finally signed off by management.

You are probably asking how my internship came about (and yes, it IS unpaid). I recently decided to take a gap year between lives, because my last one was really long. I died at 108. (When you live as long as that, a local news reporter will come by to ask you the secret of your longevity. I like to confuse them by saying, "Three mushrooms a day" or "I wash my hair in egg whites." It's one of the few pleasures available to the truly old.) If you've done an extra-long shift Down There (on Earth) you are encouraged to spend a bit more time Up Here to cool off.

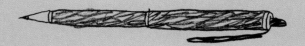

When you arrive Up Here, you get to choose your age. I always go young after a long stint on the physical plane. So now I'm nineteen again—what a relief. I was getting bored of having to dole out a dose of wisdom with every conversation. I also wasn't a fan of the incontinence.

I imagine you have a rather grand idea of what the afterlife is like, but really, it's pretty chaotic. A lot of departments are still using paper, and there aren't enough employees to do all the really important work that has to be done, so it can get a bit stressful—late nights, early mornings, that kind of thing. I get some money for lunch and travel expenses, which is more than my friend Heather gets at Condé Nast, but the social life isn't as glamorous.

I work in Check-In/Check-Out. It's a small department—just three of us at the moment—and our main responsibility is admitting people who've died and passed the test to get Up Here. They've relaxed the rules about entry since the Bible was written. These days they'll overlook low-level stuff like swearing, masturbation, or bootcut jeans. We're still strict on murder, embezzlement, and square-toed shoes though.

Our office is a small tollbooth just inside the gates, right next to Human Resources and the supply shed. Just turn right at the top of the stairs and you'll get to us—but then if you're new Up Here, you'll come see us first anyway. The Wi-Fi signal is terrible, so things can be slow. To be honest, it's a bit of a mess. Paper everywhere, a cluttered notice board on the wall (covered in pizza menus and a special offer on printer cartridges that expired three years ago), a filing cabinet with three locked drawers and no key, and one of those "Get Working. You Ain't Dead Yet" magnets. I should probably organize a bit, but there never seems to be enough time.

Gail handles Check-In. She's the first person that people see once they've passed over, so she always has nice hair, and she gets through a lot of mints that give her indigestion. New arrivals give their name at her window, she checks them against this great big ledger, assigns them a ticket, and sends them off to Orientation. It's the beginning of a long, strange journey, and they're often a little freaked out after all the dying (it never gets easier, however many times you do it). Gail confided to me during the recent staff retreat that she worries they will eventually make her job automated. She says people need to see a friendly face at this point in their journey. She has a good heart.

WELCOM
POT LUCK
Monday nights
PIL
Tuesday
Thursday
Sundays
DROP SLOT
PONG!
REC. CENTER
FRIDAYS
HAPPY HOUR
FEEDBACK FORMS
THANK YOU
CK-INS
ERE
Welcome!
BE A GEM
RETURN THE PENS

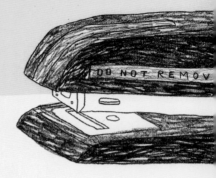

On the other side of the tollbooth is Tom, who's in charge of Check-Out. This is where people heading down to Earth for their next life are signed out. They hand in their key fob and are given an information pack: who their parents are going to be, their main goals for this life, and any emergency numbers they might need while on assignment. Tom really likes his job. Imagine a tour guide on a sightseeing bus. Now take that guide, remove the bus and the microphone, and put him in a small booth with a window. That's Tom. He says things like "Uh-oh, you again!" and "They finally kicked you out eh?" He says these things A LOT. But people always laugh.

And then there's me. I should probably explain how I ended up sitting at a small desk between Tom and Gail, with full access to their snack cupboard.

At one of the recent management meetings, there was a heated discussion about evolution. One of the new arrivals who had worked his way up the ranks pretty quickly (they say he was a big deal in computers Down There) was telling everyone about something called a "software

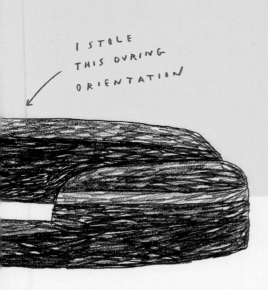

update." Apparently it happens every few months—suddenly your computer is hit with an update, and everything gets faster and more efficient. People started asking The Boss why our version of updates takes so long—hundreds of thousands of years to modify a tiny bone, or make a slight change in pelvis size, or adapt a mating ritual. They said that it's high time we upgraded a few things Down There. It got quite heated.

The Boss (who they say has been acting a bit impulsively recently) became a bit excited. He slammed his lightning bolt on the floor and BOOM! Updates are now the next big customer service project. At the office picnic the other day one of the Accounts Team members suggested He may be going through a midlife crisis, which would explain the gold cape, but His enthusiasm seems to be having an effect on all of us. Everyone's pretty fired up.

The upshot was that an Updates Team was created. The first line of business was to design a feedback form asking for any improvements or suggestions to be included in an initial round of fast-track updates. If it's successful it will become a regular feature.

So now everyone queuing at Check-In is asked if they'd like to fill in one of these forms. It gives them something to do while they wait. To be honest, I think they weren't expecting much take-up, but the response has been overwhelming. They installed a box outside the Check-In window for people to post their forms. That got filled up pretty quickly. Last month Gail finally got round to asking what she was meant to do with all the responses.

The Boss told her to send Him anything big—anything that mentions climate, or disease, or politics, or racism, or sexism—He is working on those Himself. And then He said she should get an intern to work through some of the suggestions. I was doing something dull in Accounts, so I applied and got the transfer.

I have been given carte blanche with the less important suggestions (animal stuff, a few plant things, body modifications, instinct changes— "Throw 'em a bone while I work out the big stuff," He said). I write a report on each one and send it to the Updates Team to approve (or not). I just need to look at feasibility, possible repercussions, that kind of thing. It's mostly research (and a bit of imagination).

It's a lot of responsibility for an intern, but I have good analytical skills, and I work well under pressure (plus I did a bit of drawing when I was at school). I really want to make this work—I mean, I'm interning Up Here; this could really lead somewhere.

FEEDBACK FORM

WE HAVE PUT TOGETHER A BRIEF FORM REGARDING YOUR MOST
RECENT EXISTENCE. PLEASE FILL THIS OUT AND HAND IN AT CHECK-IN.
THANK YOU!

NAME _____

CAUSE OF DEATH _____

PLEASE SELECT YOUR OVERALL LEVEL OF SATISFACTION:

	VERY SATISFIED	SOMEWHAT SATISFIED	HORRIBLE
ATMOSPHERE	☐	☐	☐
HUMAN FUNCTIONALITY	☐	☐	☐
GENERAL SERVICE	☐	☐	☐

HOW WOULD YOU RANK YOUR OVERALL EXPERIENCE EXISTING _____
ON A SCALE OF 1-10 (10 BEING "LIFE WAS AWESOME!")

DO YOU HAVE ANY SUGGESTIONS TO HELP US IMPROVE OUR
PRODUCTS AND SERVICES FOR LIVING?

Thank You

EMOTIONAL
ENGINEERING

~~~ Gravity

MORE
FLEXIBL

POS

MY N

TY
TY
ONTY

FINISH
BY 9 pm ✳

UHGRAM CHECK-IN
MEET W/ SNAKES (long meeting roo
CALL HR – Delacruz

SPATIALLY EFFICIENT	CAMOUFLAGE

BLE FIXES

GASTROPODS DEPT - EX
— 535

* RETURN TOMS CHAIR
CALL NERVES DEPT (AGAIN)
CYRIL — INSECTS CALL GO

OTES

NUMBERS

PICK UP GAIL
6 OUT FRONT

ORIENTATION
MEETING 7:00

SPEECH
879
(SPEAK LWOLF)

FELINE
DEPT.
123

HAIR
98

DEPT
EX

TE
0 0

H.R.
ask for C

ailable ?,)

SLEEP DEPARTMENT 878

uements

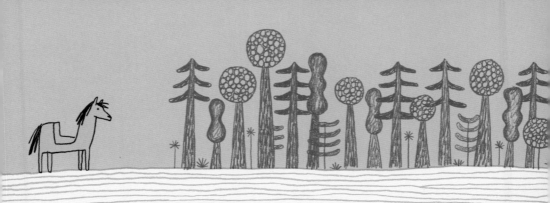

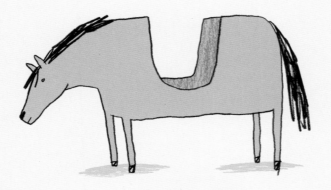

HORSES

NAME Rick Early
CAUSE OF DEATH Frisbee accident
SUBJECT OF UPGRADE Horses
REASON FOR UPGRADE It's way too easy to fall off a horse.

UPGRADE SUGGESTION I'm pretty sure there's some wiggle room to make horse riding safer. They go way back there, and then you finally get that funny old tail at the end. How about an indented back, so a rider could just slot in— no saddle, no stirrups. More comfortable for the horse too!

My initial thoughts are that this could work. I rode quite a few horses over my lives, and it's pretty hard. You've got to hold on, and tell it where to go, and make sure it's happy—a lot to think about. And you have to look sophisticated (or at least not terrified) while doing it.

Space-wise, we'll have to move some of the vital organs, but there is a lot of room to maneuver.

Who designed the camel? I checked Gail's Staff Directory and called the number for the camel guys—no answer. I left a message and I guess they will call back. I imagine they haven't been too busy recently (note: are camels due for an update?).

Anyway, back to horses. Will we need to standardize the indentation? We can't have larger people excluded. The indent will have to be narrow enough to hold the rider in snug. Let's make some breeds with a wider slot, some breeds with a narrow slot.

I settled on S, M, L, and XL. There may be scope for an extendable version if this proves popular.

Who needs to be consulted? Cowboys, police, jockeys (note: order some in XS too).

This may affect the design molds for zebras, donkeys, and mules— look into that.

Weight distribution will be different so hooves need to be looked at. Reminder: call the hoof guys.

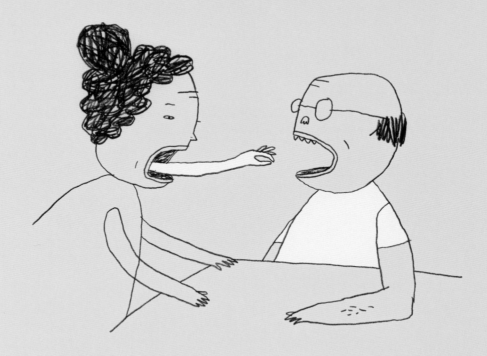

Tongue Hands

NAME Divya Khatri
CAUSE OF DEATH Julio Iglesias
SUBJECT OF UPGRADE Tongues
REASON FOR UPGRADE Food stuck in the teeth is THE WORST.

UPGRADE SUGGESTION Tongues should have a tiny hand at the end, in case the person you're kissing has something stuck in their teeth.

Not a bad idea. You would never need to use a toothpick again.

You could carry a tiny toothbrush and toothpaste in your pocket on a date, and they would have no idea you were hoping to stay over (presumption can be such a passion-killer, but so is bad breath).

Also, there's nothing worse than being in a new relationship when the other person has something in their teeth, and you don't know them well enough to tell them. With a tiny tongue hand you could just pick it out while kissing, and they'd never know.

Pros:
- You could hold tongue hands when you don't feel like kissing or holding real hands.
- Lipstick correction, nose picking—all easier.
- Great for the nail salon business, with everyone getting an extra five nails.
- You could "mouth high-five" or "mouth wave" someone if your regular hands were full. Or do the heavy metal hand signal at a concert while holding the beers.

Cons:
- Toothpick manufacturers could go out of business, unless we can bring back pineapple and cheese chunks as acceptable party food.
- Could affect dentistry. Unless you're romantically involved with your dentist, you don't want them putting their tongue in your mouth.

Call the mouth designers and Hand and Nail departments to "spitball" ideas. Do we need to move teeth? Can we get some testers onboard now? Lots of moving parts. Mouth-feel is important here.

Giant Honeybees

NAME Teddy Prink
CAUSE OF DEATH Choked on a marshmallow
SUBJECT OF UPGRADE Bees
REASON FOR UPGRADE Bees have had it bad recently. Let's cheer them up.

UPGRADE SUGGESTION Honeybees should be bigger—way bigger. Try the size of baby pandas, and fluffier. Make them really soft. The buzzing would be soothing, and just imagine the honey!

I called the Bee department, but they said they are very busy at the moment and will get back to me. I'm not so sure they will. I'll see what I can work out myself—I did pretty well with horses the other week.

We need someone who is good at physics (or whatever controls flying and stuff), who can work out how big the wings have to be if the body weight and mass are increased. I'm sure I read that they technically shouldn't be able to fly as they are—that's not going to get easier if we increase their size by 30,000 percent (or something; math has never been my strong point).

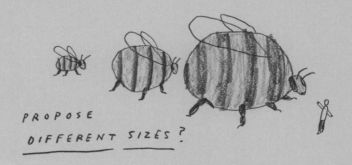

PROPOSE DIFFERENT SIZES?

FIXING FLAMINGOS

Optimal size: Feedback suggests baby panda. I'm thinking Shetland pony—then kids and smaller adults could ride them.

Have asked for some fur samples to be sent down—we want softer than dog fur but not as soft as rabbit (too slippery, hard to grip). MUST BE CUDDLY.

Concerns:
- How loud would buzzing be? Would we have to wear ear plugs?
- This will affect pollination. Do we make flowers bigger?
- How big is the queen if the worker bees are the size of ponies?
- Where do they live? Hives are going to have to change. Stingers like fencing swords could potentially cause havoc.

One upside: Beekeepers won't need to wear all that netting. A big downside: Swarms would be terrifying.

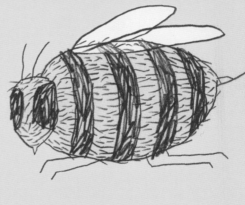

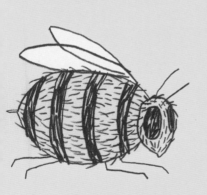

Sunsets

NAME Kip Prendle
CAUSE OF DEATH Tantra
SUBJECT OF UPGRADE Sunsets
REASON FOR UPGRADE Too predictable

UPGRADE SUGGESTION Sunsets should go sideways sometimes, just to mix things up. You should never know what you're getting. Keep you on your toes, AND impress the ladies.

I'm getting into the swing of things a bit more this week, so I thought I'd try a more challenging one.

How do we get a sunset to go sideways?

I sent an email to the Tech department, and they said it shouldn't be too hard. They've estimated a half-day programming time, but it means that sunsets will be out for one of the hemispheres. Hopefully it won't run over or people will start to notice, but maybe we could time it with a natural disaster. Note: Check with Geology to find out if any volcanoes are on schedule to erupt soon.

Concerns
- Will sideways sunsets cause neck injuries?
- Where will the sun actually go?
- Will it mess up circadian rhythms? Schedule a meeting with someone in Body Clocks.
- What impact on song lyrics? I don't think any currently mention the sun going "left."

Update: Tech messed up and the sun only goes left to right now. They have promised they will get it fixed ASAP (apparently three of the team are going to do overtime today) but I'm really worried someone will notice.

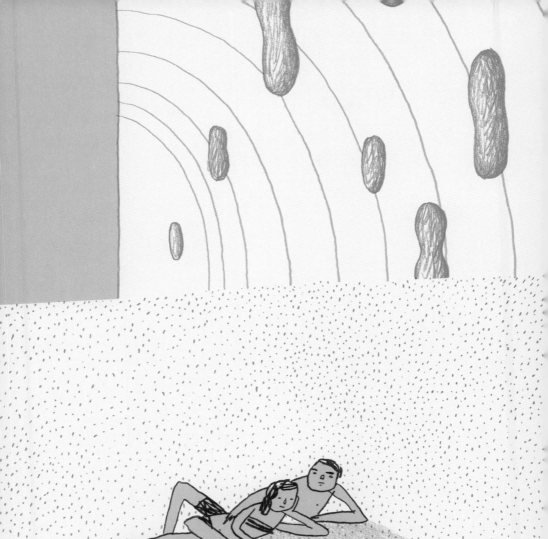

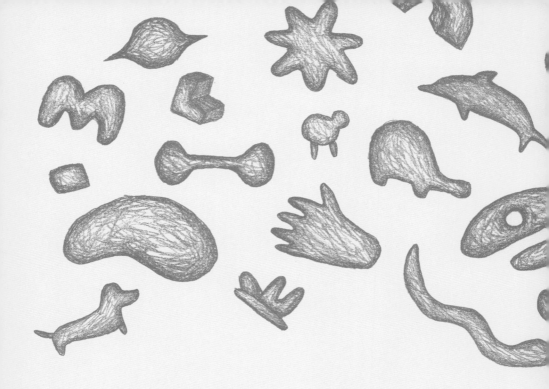

Clouds

NAME Peter Thorpe

CAUSE OF DEATH Tightrope accident

SUBJECT OF UPGRADE Clouds

REASON FOR UPGRADE Design coherence

UPGRADE SUGGESTION There are too many badly designed clouds. How about four hundred really stylish humdingers that go on tour around the world? You could try and see them all before you die.

This is one of my favorites so far. I agree with Peter: I've seen some really poorly thought-out clouds, just scattered scraps across the sky, then poof. Gone. And never any kind of theme or continuity.

We could make it interactive: Issue a booklet at birth and if you get to cross out all of them in your lifetime you win a prize (a plaque for your house, or a digital radio. I've just invented Cloud Bingo).

It's imperative that this is fair, if we are offering prizes. Each cloud must pass over each country at least a few times a year. Sweden can't get all the clouds in a month and LA get nothing.

I called the original designer, who sounded a bit defensive on the phone. She said it's not her fault; she designed them "before everyone had a camera in their pocket all the damn time." I recommended we take this off her hands and she didn't protest.

Concerns:
- We are going to need a reputable designer for this. Check recent arrivals for anyone big in fashion or art.
- Find out if we can recycle the current cloud stock—this should help keep costs down.
- Will they need to be coated in something to keep the shape?
- Will that affect birds/air traffic/rain?
- Can airplanes still fly through them?
- Should we keep them white or is it time for a new color palette? We don't want them to clash with the sky.

Frogs

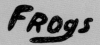

NAME Francesco Morales
CAUSE OF DEATH Capoeira fight
SUBJECT OF UPGRADE Frogs
REASON FOR UPGRADE I'm bored.

UPGRADE SUGGESTION Move frogs up the food chain. They are pretty to look at but they don't really do anything. Our village had a lot of frogs and I used to watch them for hours. It was so boring. Slightly less boring than not watching them, but still boring.

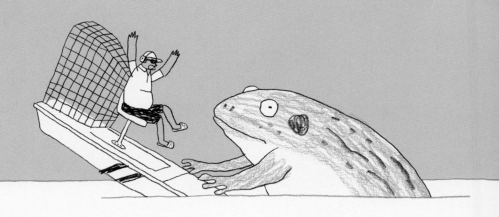

I've booked an afternoon to familiarize myself with the Food Chain ledger. Need to work out where frogs currently sit. So far it looks like they're above dragonflies, but under nearly everyone else.

- Where do we want them to be? Tougher than rodents? Can they kill gerbils? Ducks? Dogs?
- We will need to upgrade their digestive system if they're going to become full-blown carnivores—could copy the cat one.
- We'll need to add sharp teeth and claws.
- Speed? Jumping will add an element of surprise.
- Do we want to include a squeeze action like a python?
- How does this impact French cuisine?
- What about fairytales? We can't have love-sick princesses getting their faces bitten off.

I think I'll decide what they will eat and then work out how they will kill it—basically work backward. So, if frogs can kill badgers, then we need a viable badger-killing technique. Biting? Poison? Swallowing whole?

I'm going to park this one for a while. It seems like a lot of work just because one guy couldn't be bothered to take up a hobby or read a book.

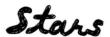

Stars

NAME Ariel Dujean
CAUSE OF DEATH Spontaneous combustion
SUBJECT OF UPGRADE Stars
REASON FOR UPGRADE No longer relevant

UPGRADE SUGGESTION The stars need to move into new constellations because these ones make no sense to a modern audience. Orion's Belt is literally three dots. People are more sophisticated now.

Competition idea: Give high school students worldwide twenty stars each and ask them to come up with a new constellation. Then do a big reveal with winning results shared live in a Eurovision-type event. Hang on, that won't work. I keep forgetting we can't let on about Up Here, Down There.

I agree constellations need to be more modern and culturally relevant for a global audience.

Some ideas:
- The cell phone charger
- Emojis (poop, eggplant, smiley face)
- The take-out coffee cup
- Keanu Reeves

Alternatively, we could make them educational:
- The Lifecycle of the Crane Fly
- The Battle of Hastings
- The Venn Diagram

Concerns:
- How does this affect astrology?
- What happens when someone who's happy being a Pisces suddenly finds they're a Designer Sneaker?

Love Noise

NAME Philippe Mathis
CAUSE OF DEATH Necktie fire
SUBJECT OF UPGRADE Romantic love
REASON FOR UPGRADE Awkwardness

UPGRADE SUGGESTION You've recently met someone, and things are going well. But you don't want to say "I love you" first. What if they don't say it back? The whole affair—and your self-esteem—is ruined. I propose an alarm that goes off when you have both realized you are in love. No more stress, no more tears.

This must have happened a lot for Philippe to put this in his feedback form. It's a good idea, although surely some of the excitement of romance is not knowing if the other person feels the same way?

It needs to be loud—what if it happens when they're in a nightclub, and the music drowns it out? It should probably happen a few times over subsequent days to ensure that both parties have definitely registered it.

Where would the alarm be located?

How about an involuntary shout? Or a long, loud hiccup. That way both of them would be aware it has happened, and we could use the voice box and existing noisemaking structures. Much cheaper than adding an alarm or Klaxon to the body.

It's very important that the sound can't be replicated by someone wanting to see how the other person feels. And it MUST BE un-hackable.

Potential problems with extramarital affairs. Imagine if Philippe is having an affair with his wife's sister, and both couples are having dinner. A glance passes between the two adulterers—love noise goes off, everyone knows, dinner is ruined before the cheese course.

We could have a stipulation that it can only happen when the couple in question is alone. A mute option? Signs for the hard of hearing?

Pros:
People can't lie about their feelings.

Cons:
People can't lie about their feelings.

Will this cause more distress? You've been dating someone for five years and still no noise. You know you love them, but they obviously don't feel the same. What is your cutoff point?

What about someone whose alarm never goes off? It wouldn't just affect people who have never felt love, it would be awful for those unlucky people who have never had love returned. That's really sad.

I've had a few days to think on this and I'm not sure this one should go ahead. Love is a minefield already and I think this causes more problems than it solves. I'm sorry, Philippe, it's not you, it's me (it is you though).

Talking Dogs / Cats

NAME Mariam Goldstein
CAUSE OF DEATH Shrimp cocktail
SUBJECT OF UPGRADE Dogs and cats
REASON FOR UPGRADE Education

UPGRADE SUGGESTION Dogs must talk. We need to hear what they are thinking. Cats must not talk. We must never hear what they are thinking.

This is a popular one, I've seen a few dog talking requests. But this must be handled carefully. Dogs don't go through "the forgetting" between lives (mandatory for all other species), so they know everything while they're Down There. Think about that next time you pet one. It knows EVERYTHING. And this is why they're not able to speak to humans. As we all know, dogs are notoriously bad at keeping secrets.

Is there a way of allowing dogs to speak, but only on certain subjects? Food, walkies, cricket?

Would they get around this? Some of the brainier breeds, like sheepdogs, are not going to be fooled by language restrictions.

Can the canine voice box switch from woofs to words? Must contact the tongue people. If dogs get human tongues, they may get more sensitive palates and not be able to eat dog food anymore. And what about their grooming routines? I'm not sure we should be increasing their capacity for taste, considering where their tongues spend a lot of their time.

Do we want them to sound like humans? Could be a bit freaky. What would a dog's voice sound like? Would they have accents?

RE CATS: Mariam is spot on here—we can't do talking cats. They tried something similar years ago but decided against it because of what happened during the testing phase. A number of researchers on the project ended up being signed off work for stress, and the department had to run self-esteem workshops for a few years before everyone resumed their jobs. Let's not go there again.

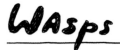

Wasps

NAME Jaroslav Grzanecki
CAUSE OF DEATH Beer pong
SUBJECT OF UPGRADE Wasps
REASON FOR UPGRADE The devil makes work for idle wings.

UPGRADE SUGGESTION Wasps need a job. Bees have something to do. Even flies serve a purpose. But wasps just ruin picnics, and I can do that perfectly well myself.

We have a Jobs Board up here. It's mostly used by the Parasite Team—a lot of vacancies come up for blood suckers, or bugs that clean an elephant's ears, something to burrow inside a snail and eat it from the inside, that kind of thing.

There wasn't anything that jumped out at me when I looked for something suitable for the wasp. I don't think they are great at cleaning (they do have six limbs, but none of them can hold a sponge), and they're useless at languages (what's buzz in French anyway?).

I dug out the Wasp resume, and it had this listed under "Skills":
- Flying
- Stinging
- Persistence
- Stinging
- Determination
- Microsoft Excel (competent)
- Buzzing
- Stinging
- Aggression

A couple of things come to mind that would be ideal for a swarm of wasps:
- Nightclub bouncers
- Security for politicians/celebrities
- Guarding valuables
- Admin

If we took the sting out, we could give them:
- Clothing for people whose clothes have suddenly fallen off
- Fun, noisy toupee
- Flash mobs (hello, 2005)

I'll have to come back to this. My mind has gone blank. They can wait anyway, the stingy little bastards.

FiNGERnaiLs

NAME Jim Cutler
CAUSE OF DEATH Poisoned Slush Puppie
SUBJECT OF UPGRADE Fingernails
REASON FOR UPGRADE Excess

UPGRADE SUGGESTION Too many fingernails! We really only need one fingernail per person—for picking at tape/undoing knots/scratching backs. Beats me why we have to have ten of the buggers.

Right. If we are removing nine nails, we need to look into whether we are replacing them with anything. Does the skin from the rest of the finger just carry on where the nail used to be? Does it need to be coated in something a bit tougher, like a steel cap on a boot? Or, um, a nail?

Which finger should get the nail? Instinct would say index finger of the dominant hand, but maybe that's useful for other things. Maybe it should be a middle finger—it doesn't do much apart from insult people.

How will this affect guitar playing? Nail salons? Nail biters and anxiety? If there is only one nail, should we add some extra features?

- Extendable—to reach things high up, or to clean someone else's ear
- Retractable—to pretend you didn't just clean someone's ear
- Extra-sharp—for cutting prosciutto

Concerns:

- High probability they will become status symbols, with tribal leaders and rappers and business tycoons growing extra-long single nails. That's going to be annoying.
- What about toes? Has anyone mentioned toenails yet? I'll come back to this when I've checked the rest of the forms, because we could do them together.

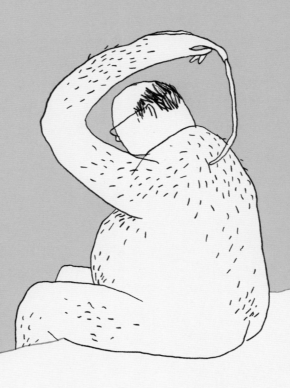

FEET

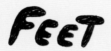

NAME Linda Fernandez
CAUSE OF DEATH Cat flu
SUBJECT OF UPGRADE Feet
REASON FOR UPGRADE Shoe prices

UPGRADE SUGGESTION Everyone should have the same size feet, so we can wear each other's shoes. It would be a lot cheaper if families just had 'family shoes' that everyone could wear. Plus, if we could actually walk a mile in each other's shoes, instead of just talking about it, maybe we'd understand each other a little better. But mostly the money thing.

I have a feeling Linda had larger feet than her friends. It was the same for me. Could never borrow any of my friends' shoes until I found a foot-twin in college. We didn't even get on that well, but we stayed friends until the end. Actually, I'm pretty sure she's still got my pink Birkenstocks.

A universal, all-age foot size, regardless of height and sex—it's very egalitarian, but would it actually work in practice?

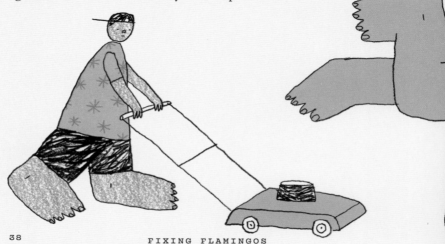

Pros:
- Shoes never get too small
- Children fall over less
- No more of those antiquated shoe rulers at the Payless store

Cons:
- I actually can't think of any
- Oh: Clowns. They will be pissed.

Babies should not be born with adult feet—sets up all sorts of birth-canal issues. I recommend an enlargement at about one year old. From that day on, the child can wear any of the household shoes.

This shouldn't be too hard to implement.

Send request to Podiatry for the midsize foot blueprint and apply it to all DNA, and coding that it should happen at Birthday 1.

Should it happen gradually, or suddenly, overnight? If we could spread it over a month or two it would reduce the chance of freaking out both child and parents. Or I could get the Copywriting Team to draft a nursery story about a foot fairy that visits in the middle of the night. Make it a rite of passage.

Choose date of universal rollout.

Just received a message from upstairs—all foot-related updates to go straight to The Boss. Wonder what that's about.

NAME Almila Yilmaz
CAUSE OF DEATH Unrequited love
SUBJECT OF UPGRADE Eggs
REASON FOR UPGRADE Convenience

UPGRADE SUGGESTION Chickens in hot countries should lay hard-boiled eggs.

Pretty self-explanatory. Obviously not all eggs, as some eggs are used to create more chickens. And omelets. A percentage could be hard-boiled, however.

This mustn't be exploited.

How about this: Chickens can only lay hard-boiled eggs (or any eggs, for that matter) if they're really happy. Farms will have to be the happiest places in the world in order for there to be any yield at all.

What would a chicken's happy place look like?

- I've seen YouTube videos of chickens playing piano, so an array of musical instruments that can be played with beaks
- Slides
- Paddling pools
- Worms on sushi-style conveyor belts
- Cubby holes
- Dust bowls

Chickens reach the required level of happiness, then bingo! They lay an egg.

We need to roll this out to all animal farming. I'd love to see farmers reading to their dairy cows, for example.

However, this isn't Almila's main request. I'll need to speak to one of the engineers about this. I know chickens get pretty hot when they are incubating their eggs in a nest, so maybe we just make that happen sooner, allowing them to boil them before laying.

BUTTERFLIES

NAME Kirsten Baumgartner
CAUSE OF DEATH Hot yoga
SUBJECT OF UPGRADE Butterflies
REASON FOR UPGRADE Unfair representation

UPGRADE SUGGESTION I worked in a bookshop selling tarot cards and spiritual books, and I saw A LOT of butterfly art. Are butterflies happy being the "poster insect" of transformation? If they were a bit more vicious, maybe people would leave them off the Reiki workbooks, and let someone else have a chance.

Vicious butterflies would surely shake things up a bit. This could be fun. We could start with some fangs, claws, a taste for blood. I'd like to see a sharp, serrated edge around the wings so they could do some damage while flying. While we're on that, enough with the fluttering. If they're going to up their killing game, they'll need to be able to dive bomb their enemy. Which, if we do this right, will be everybody.

How do we make butterflies the assholes of the insect world? We'll leave the caterpillar as it is, eating leaves and cupcakes and watermelons. Let's look at the chrysalis phase. How does our caterpillar feel, facing its next stage? We need to foster some resentment. Hard done by for having to go through a huge and potentially disturbing transformation? Maybe it wanted to stay wandering about as a larva but no, THAT wasn't good enough. Society told it that it had to become the Elton John of insects.

"Why wasn't I OK as I was? Why did you only love me once I became pretty? I didn't ask for any of this!" (We should add an extra dose of big teenager energy.)

This resentment and self-pity fuels an unquenchable thirst for revenge.

The butterfly emerges. It's beautiful, but it's a real bitch. It has sharp claws. It has deadly fangs. It has some kind of poison (check with Environmental Health and Safety if this is a good idea). It has serrated wings. And it has a score to settle.

Concerns:
• How does this impact tattoos?

DANCiNG

NAME Barry Weaver
CAUSE OF DEATH Hair dye allergy
SUBJECT OF UPGRADE Dancing
REASON FOR UPGRADE Equality

UPGRADE SUGGESTION Bad dancing should become good dancing; good dancing should become bad dancing.

Request definitions of Good and Bad dancing (with demonstrations) from *Soul Train* host Don Cornelius (pretty sure he's still here).

This is a simple perception switch, where we pretend something that was previously unacceptable is now the height of desirability. We did something similar with nerds and popular girls a few years ago and that worked out well (until the "Zuckerberg situation" ruined it). Also, the 1970s. There's no way that decade happened without someone flipping a switch.

Concerns:
• Weddings—will they be more or less fun?

More people will be good dancers, so they'll be more likely to participate. But that also means there will only be one or two "bad" dancers per wedding, so fewer people to laugh at.

Shoulders

NAME Chris Harrison
CAUSE OF DEATH Big Bird
SUBJECT OF UPGRADE Length of shoulders
REASON FOR UPGRADE Efficiency

UPGRADE SUGGESTION One shoulder should be wider for carrying all the stuff you need for a family beach day.

According to Chris's registration file, he had seven kids, so this must have been a pressing concern for him.

I'm going to base my calculations on a more restrained family size: two kids and two adults.

For one beach day a family of four would need the following:
- 2 pail and shovel sets
- 2 cooler bags of drinks and food
- 1 large bag of towels
- A selection of picnic chairs or blankets
- 2 sets of water wings or inflatable floaties (uninflated)
- 1 bag containing swimwear and a warm option for each family member
- 1 bag of diapers, baby stuff (depending on age of family members)
- 1 large umbrella or alternative shade option
- 1 bag of sunscreen, first-aid items
- And for Chris, being in California, a surfboard

If we allocated four inches for each item on an arm (this will need to be properly tested by the Mathematics department) we are looking at a single shoulder width of around five feet. Of course, this is assuming that one adult is carrying the above, and the other is making sure the children don't escape/get run over/drown.

Need to look at balance, exercise equipment, and official school photo dimensions. Will it be the same side for everyone, or will some people be left-shouldered and some right-shouldered?

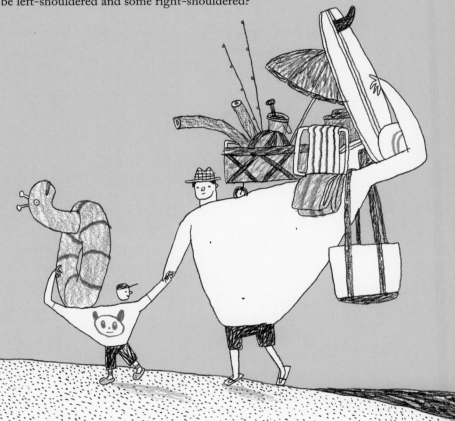

Clothes will have to be redesigned. Cars will need to be widened—planes, buses, trains too.

The sport of diving won't survive, but tennis will become more interesting.

Turnstiles are fine.

Revolving doors will be unusable.

Laughing

NAME Kevin Willbond
CAUSE OF DEATH Sausages
SUBJECT OF UPGRADE Laughing
REASON FOR UPGRADE Taking people down a peg (or two)

UPGRADE SUGGESTION Laughing at someone should reduce your height by half an inch each time.

OK Kevin. Lots to unpack here.

This would have to start in adulthood, because children are always laughing at each other. They'd never make it to five feet otherwise.

It should only happen if you are maliciously laughing at someone, not for good-natured laughing with someone, or else comedy audiences would be tiny.

What would happen if you saw someone walk into a lamppost, and you didn't want to laugh because you knew it was wrong, but you couldn't help it? Shortening in this case would be unfair. We would need a caveat that immediate remorse cancels out the process.

Also, some people deserve to be laughed at. Politicians, for example. If we shortened everyone who laughed at them on a daily basis, the world's population would be the size of skittles within a month.

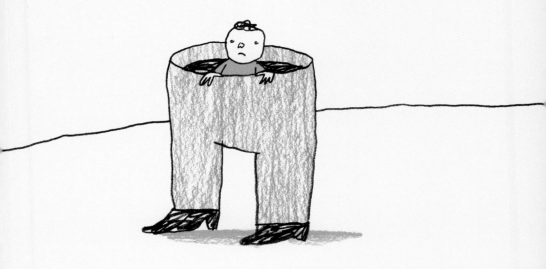

Put in a call to the organs and nervous system coordinators: How condensed can someone be and still have a fully functioning bodily system?

If we just compress someone by half an inch, they become denser—we need to involve the Physics Team (I think this is physics again, right?).

As an incentive for good behavior people could regain height by doing something good. Like offsetting flights with a carbon tax. Although we'd have to avoid richer people "buying" the privilege to laugh at others.

TEETH

NAME Godfrey Orji
CAUSE OF DEATH Hysteria
SUBJECT OF UPGRADE Teeth
REASON FOR UPGRADE Unsatisfactory design

UPGRADE SUGGESTION Teeth are a nightmare. Why do kids lose them? It's horrible. Babies should be born with a full set of adult teeth that stay perfectly healthy throughout their lives. Brushing is nice so let's keep doing that, but flossing and root canals are a total waste of time and money. Also teeth should also be stronger—like open doors stronger.

Godfrey makes some really good points here.

Why do kids lose their teeth? I agree, it's horrible. First the realization that it's wobbling, and then the urge to waggle it with your tongue when it's all dangly and hanging by a thread but you're not brave enough to pull it out. In fact, it's one of the things I look forward to least when starting a new life. If we were born with a full set of unbreakable, healthy adult teeth, that would take out a huge chunk of the misery of being a child. It would look creepy, but babies look creepy anyway.

How does this impact the tooth fairy, and childhood economics in general?

Healthy teeth all the time—this will put dentists out of business. Do we need dentists? Is there another profession that will satisfy people with this unique skill set? Do they enjoy inflicting pain, or do they just like talking to people who can't answer back? Is it the chair? If so, we could easily move them over to hairdressing or minor plastic surgery.

They should be "open doors stronger." This is a good idea. If you're catering an event and entering a room with a full dinner tray, you could use your teeth to open the door. Gardening and DIY would be easier as the teeth could dig, weed, or remove tricky nails in planks, while your hands play piano or knit a sweater behind your back.

GETTING OLDER

NAME Ethel Rabinowitz
CAUSE OF DEATH Speedboat crash
SUBJECT OF UPGRADE Aging
REASON FOR UPGRADE It would be fun!

UPGRADE SUGGESTION We get better looking as we get older, so by the time we are in our eighties we're knockouts.

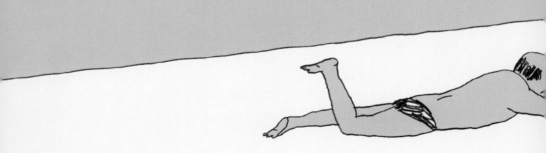

Aging is handled by the Rotary Club members (they took over when Father Time retired), so I need to schedule a meeting with them. It's another coding issue, but there will be serious sociological repercussions we need to keep in mind.

First, let's keep fertility as it is. We don't want people becoming parents in their nineties.

If we keep getting better looking, does that mean we essentially slow down the process of reaching our sexual peak? Or does it mean that humans will just continue getting better and better looking, eventually attaining unprecedented levels of hotness? Is that even safe?

I'll need some renderings and 3D models from the Production department.

On the plus side, there would be a lot more to look forward to as we age, and if we are lucky enough to enjoy a leisurely retirement, we'll have better things to do with our time than gardening and watching reruns of *Murder She Wrote*.

Concerns:
- Some people find the end of their sexual years as a relief (I know I did, but that might have been because my husband lived so bloody long). It could be a drag, having to keep up with lingerie trends and dating apps.
- Will no one do puzzles anymore?
- It will be the end of knitting.

Eyes Eating

NAME Yannis Papakonstantinou
CAUSE OF DEATH Esophageal obstruction (pistachio nut)
SUBJECT OF UPGRADE Eyes
REASON FOR UPGRADE Increased eating abilities (I love food)

UPGRADE SUGGESTION You can smile with your eyes—why can't you eat with your eyes?

I've sent a request up to the relevant departments to see if it's possible to ingest food through the eyes. I can't see anything solid working. Or anything hot. What does that leave—gazpacho and yogurt?

Will we be able to taste through the eyes, or is this just a way to curb hunger?

Will we still be able to see, or will eating induce temporary blindness?

Restaurants would have to provide the relevant cutlery for food that is ingested ocularly.

Food could get stuck in eyelashes instead of beards.

It would help with eating and talking at the same time. At least we wouldn't have to look at someone's half-masticated fishcakes while they're telling us all about their day at work. But is that any worse than watching them feed noodles into their eyeballs?

Positive: You could kiss someone while eating without tasting their food.

Negative: You'd be more at risk of being mugged if your eyes were full of spaghetti bolognese.

What if you started crying at dinner?

Greedy people might eat with their eyes and their mouth at the same time.

This has thrown up way too many questions (could you throw up from your eyes? Let's not). I think this is going to be more trouble than it's worth. I'm not sure Yannis is taking this seriously.

Memory Clean Up

NAME Yulia Dabrowska
CAUSE OF DEATH Boredom
SUBJECT OF UPGRADE Memory storage
REASON FOR UPGRADE Insufficient capacity

UPGRADE SUGGESTION The option to clean up my memory. I didn't need to remember the lyrics to that Def Leppard song. They took up valuable space that could have been used for storing my kids' birthdays, or what I went into the kitchen for.

I like this. However, it's important to leave the decisions on what gets stored and what gets deleted to the individual. Otherwise, we could end up with some embarrassing situations (especially for Def Leppard tribute bands). I feel this is something we could run while asleep. Each birthday could be a good time to do it (once you're over sixteen, or eighteen? I wouldn't trust children to know what to delete).

We must ensure it's only extraneous information that is deletable. And we can't allow people to forget things they did while drunk—general bad behavior, or embarrassments—living with shame and guilt can be a good deterrent for future misdeeds.

We need categories of things that can be deleted. The following are some suggestions:
- Song lyrics
- Redundant phone numbers
- Past addresses

- Seeing your parents having sex
- Poems you were forced to learn at school but never liked
- Celebrity romances
- Out-of-date passwords
- Random names (I've had "Rimsky-Korsakov" stuck in my head since the 1890s)

On your fortieth birthday you should be allowed to clear out all the information you learned at school but never used (geometry, algebra, Latin), which will free up space for all the adult learning courses you will be taking up in middle age (local history, French cuisine, life coaching).

This would also allow all the hot eighty-year-olds to remember the names of all the people they're dating.

HoRses (again)

NAME Toby
CAUSE OF DEATH Sugar lump overdose
SUBJECT OF UPGRADE Riders
REASON FOR UPGRADE Fairness

UPGRADE SUGGESTION It's time for people to be ridden by horses.

Toby was a horse, so I can see where this came from. (It also explains why it took me ages to decipher his hoof-writing—looping bubble letters, no crossed T's—what a mess. NOTE: ping Animal Communications to review equine penmanship.)

I agree that it's time to turn the tables—although we will have to put the brakes on the update to horses' backs, if we tackle this one. It may have to go to a vote (between Gail and Tom, if I am to be completely honest).

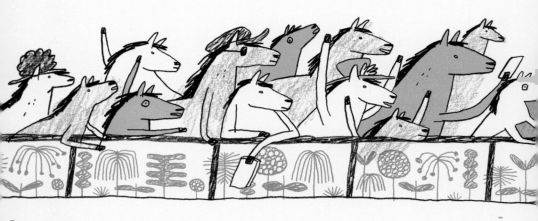

We are going to need some good mathematicians on this. We have to work out the maximum amount of weight a person can carry on their back.

Even though the numbers haven't come back yet, I can safely say that horses are going to have to be a lot smaller. They could stay the same design, but hooves would need something like a Velcro pad down the inner edge. That way the horse could wrap its front legs over the person's shoulders and the back legs around the person's waist. It seems like that could be pretty snug—and the head could face forward next to the person's head, allowing for conversation, motivation, and apple sharing.

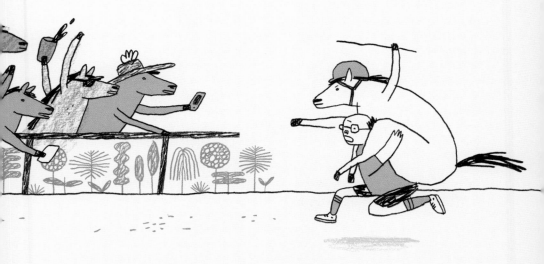

We need to get some physicists (them again) on it—if the human can't run quickly, is anyone going to watch the race? I can only imagine walking pretty slowly with a horse on my back, even a small one, so I really need to find out what is possible. And we can't make the horses too small, or it would just look like racing while wearing backpacks, and that's not going to work on TV.

We need to get the right balance between horse size and human speed, otherwise no one is going to be up for this adaptation, I'm afraid, Toby.

Mosquitos

NAME Lisimba Gondwe
CAUSE OF DEATH Shopping
SUBJECT OF UPGRADE Mosquitos
REASON FOR UPGRADE Medical needs

UPGRADE SUGGESTION Mosquitos need to start giving back. They should take blood from people who are healthy and give it to sick people.

What a brilliant idea! Mosquitos have just been troublemakers for too long. I like this idea—the Robin Hood mosquito, stealing [blood] from the [blood] rich and giving to the [blood] poor. But could it work?

It's important to add here that The Boss is already working on malaria, so for the purpose of these calculations we have to assume that He has sorted it out, and mosquitos can no longer transmit disease.

They'd have to be employed in hospitals because we can't allow them to go around taking people's blood and giving it to other people willy-nilly. That could be disastrous. We can't leave anything up to mosquitos that requires a moral compass, because they don't have one, and they're too cumbersome to install (they're way bulkier than your standard compass, and less useful).

To do any good their blood-carrying capacity is also going to have to increase massively. They'll need to be redesigned to hold at least a pint of blood to be of any use. Maybe a set of panniers on either side? They will have to be bigger, of course, so do we really want mosquitos the size of golden retrievers? And if they're working in hospitals, we have to find a way for them to wear white coats, which is going to be a struggle due to the lack of shoulders.

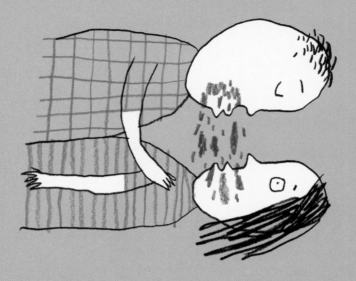

Food Kiss

NAME Jamie Kerzner
CAUSE OF DEATH Space Hopper collision
SUBJECT OF UPGRADE Food distribution
REASON FOR UPGRADE Etiquette

UPGRADE SUGGESTION You should always kiss people with a small bit of food in your mouth as a gift. It's only polite.

When The Boss started this project, I think He was hoping the feedback would concern straightforward physical updates, rather than behavioral ones. But He said we can include a few suggestions like this if we categorize them as Instinct Updates, which gives us a bit of leeway. Let's look at this one.

Firstly, it's a bit gross, I'm not going to lie. I don't want to think about the kind of person Jamie was (is), and whether he used to do this "off-piste." If he just wanted to be polite, he could have bought flowers, or complimented someone's outfit.

This throws up (sorry) all kinds of issues, such as what happens if someone is a vegan, and the person they are kissing has a nice morsel of brisket waiting for them. Or what if you're on a diet? And would it have to be every kiss? Because that would be exhausting, not to mention impossible to do if you weren't hungry.

It would change the atmosphere in restaurants, for sure.

Those annoying couples who engage in public displays of affection at every opportunity might end up with digestive issues. That could be kind of funny. But I think this is disgusting, really, and I'm going to put it in the wastepaper basket under Tom's half-eaten croissant, and pretend I never received it.

NB: This would work really well with tongue hands, if we end up going with that.

Rain Songs

NAME Lorelei Madagascar
CAUSE OF DEATH Abseiling
SUBJECT OF UPGRADE Musical rain
REASON FOR UPGRADE No reason

UPGRADE SUGGESTION Could rain sing songs? Everything else Down There was pretty cool, but I'd love to hear what that would sound like.

I like the sound of Lorelei. She doesn't really mind either way, but it's an interesting suggestion and worth looking into. She can take it or leave it.

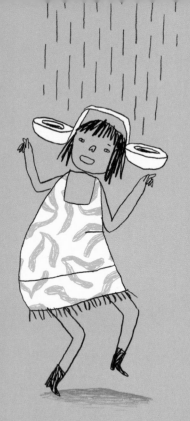

I imagine she had a nice, relaxing last life, and I wish her well.

So, singing rain. In the positive column, a lot of people find rain dreary (hello, Scotland) so a musical accompaniment would brighten things up a bit. I imagine people would join in and pretty soon everyone would be dancing about like in a 1940s musical.

However, there are more negatives lurking here. Firstly, what songs? How many would there be in rotation? Imagine if it was the same song, over and over again. Monsoon season would be unbearable. Secondly, people have a lot of different tastes, so how do you keep everyone happy? Answer: you can't. A jazz tune would upset the death metal fans. Hip-hop would annoy the opera buffs. It would be impossible.

Hell, Tom said people Down There are still disagreeing on whether toilet paper should hang over or under (over, obviously), so they're not ready to unite on something as serious as this. I would really like to live in a world where this would be possible, but until The Boss has made some pretty serious changes to the human psyche, I think we will have to put lovely Lorelei's suggestion in the Maybe pile.

Earlobes

NAME Betty Waardenburg
CAUSE OF DEATH Peanut butter addiction
SUBJECT OF UPGRADE Earlobes
REASON FOR UPGRADE What if you get lost in the wilderness?

UPGRADE SUGGESTION Earlobes should have a small pouch for snacks and coins.

At the current size, an earlobe pouch could possibly hold one really small coin, a small mint, or a piece of gum. It wouldn't be worth it.

Can we enlarge the earlobe to hold more items? I called the Ear department but they didn't pick up—Gail said it's best to email them. I asked for an earlobe design that could accommodate the following items:

- A credit card
- A handful of raisins (good energy snack)
- 10 potato chips (something salty)
- An isotonic energy sachet (for dehydration)
- A spare door key

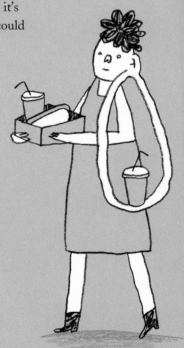

Of course, people will end up carrying useless tat in their earlobes, like a nice pebble, a photo of Britney Spears, or a bunch of old receipts, but I can only do so much.

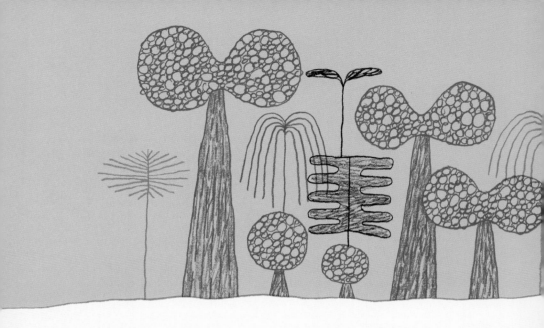

RUNNing

NAME Hector Discoball
CAUSE OF DEATH Pride
SUBJECT OF UPGRADE Running
REASON FOR UPGRADE It would be funnier.

UPGRADE SUGGESTION When people run, they should lift their knees above their heads, and their arms should be held straight out, motionless. Like a crucifix desperately running through quicksand.

The only reason Hector wants us to do this is that we would find it funny for a while. But what he doesn't know is that after a generation or two, we would all get used to it. The joke wears off. And then it wouldn't be funny anymore. It would be normal.

This is how sneezing started—it was a practical joke by one of the engineers Up Here. Everyone had a good laugh, and then we forgot about it. No one ever reset it, and now everyone sneezes as if there is a reason for it. We still laugh at some sneezes—the little "choo" ones, and the big "haaaaarrruuuummpppphhh" can sometimes raise a snigger. But they've gone mainstream, so they're no longer interesting.

And don't get me started on sex. Although we are still laughing at that one.

Baby Faces

NAME Nikolay Mihailov
CAUSE OF DEATH Duel
SUBJECT OF UPGRADE Babies
REASON FOR UPGRADE No reason! Honestly!

UPGRADE SUGGESTION Babies should be born looking exactly like the father's best friend, so the parents know who to ask to be godfather.

Obviously this can't be approved. For one thing, not all the cultures Down There incorporate the godparent model. It does make The Boss laugh when He hears about some of the things people fall for. He always sniggers when a new religion is invented. He says things like "Way off the mark! But they'll find out soon enough," which would be terrifying if He didn't have such a friendly face (and such amusing outfits).

I also have a sneaking suspicion that Nikolay was trying to hide something with this suggestion. I wonder how many babies were born looking suspiciously like Nikolay.

We got a new shredder today! So maybe it's time to try it out.

Bye bye, Nikolay.

FLAMINGOS

NAME Bishnu Gurung
CAUSE OF DEATH Tangled in hammock
SUBJECT OF UPGRADE Flamingos
REASON FOR UPGRADE They look ridiculous.

UPGRADE SUGGESTION Who the hell designed flamingos?
They need to be looked at. Great color, but nightmare
proportions with those silly legs and backward knees. Just
makes no sense.

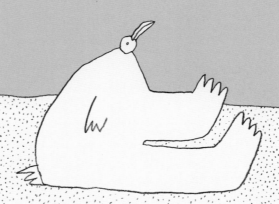

I asked the Bird department to dig out the original files for flamingos. I didn't hear anything back for ages, and it was only after a lot of pestering that the folder finally appeared on my desk.

There was just one torn piece of lined paper inside, with a crayon drawing of a long pink bird, signed "Bebe Delacruz, 7½" on it. An APPROVED stamp was on the paper.

I cross-checked the approval date with HR, and it was the first (and only, it turns out) "bring your kid to work" day.

I asked around and there was an Alvaro Delacruz who worked in bird design ages ago, and he had a daughter called Bebe. My guess is that Bebe, inspired while sitting at her dad's desk, got into the design spirit and worked up a version of flamingos using some fat crayons.

It's easy to see how this could have happened. Bird design is one of the most exciting fields to work in here, but they are always so busy.

So how do we fix flamingos? According to the diagram the knees are actually ankles, but they're way too high up. They have knees at the tops of their thighs—Bebe had drawn them in blue with an arrow. This is just too silly. Obviously they're too thin—they need much sturdier legs to hold up that body. The rest is fine, if a little odd (that's a very curly beak and having to drink with your head upside down can't be fun, we could sort that out) but I actually really like the color. In fact, more things should be that color, so I'm going to save the swatch in case I want to use it on something else.

I'm going to handle this one myself. Flamingos weren't meant to exist like that anyway, so it's really more a case of correcting rather than updating. I've seen it done enough times to know it's a simple leg width program change and a beak modification.

APPROVED
knees
Bebe Delacruz
7½

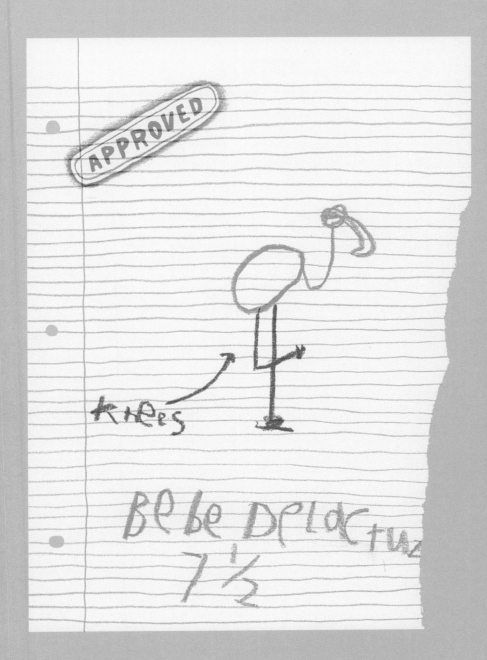

Leaf Design

NAME Angela Morrison
CAUSE OF DEATH Cookies
SUBJECT OF UPGRADE Leaf design
REASON FOR UPGRADE Lack of variation

UPGRADE SUGGESTION Leaves are so boring. Most of them are green, and they're all the same. So some are long and some are round, big deal! Surely there's something else you can do with them?

I have to agree with Angela—most leaves are green. The Leaf Team said it's something to do with chlorophyll, so I've asked them to order chlorophyll in more colors. Honestly, some people refuse to think outside the box.

While we're waiting for that, I've come up with some alternative shapes:

- One giant leaf coming out of the tree trunk—it could be quite fun to watch it turn in autumn, although you'll want to be careful when it falls
- Spheres, cubes, and pyramids
- Hands and fingers—other body parts? Too human-centric?
- Pasta shapes—especially the bow-tie ones
- Fish
- Cars of the twentieth century
- The face of the person who planted it

We could make it interactive—companies could design the leaves of the trees they sponsor. We could have Coca Cola bottles, or cell phones, or dog chews, with the money going back into tree innovation.

LABias

NAME Freddie Tarantino
CAUSE OF DEATH Bong malfunction
SUBJECT OF UPGRADE Genitalia (female)
REASON FOR UPGRADE Fairness

UPGRADE SUGGESTION Labias clap when a woman finds someone attractive.

I note that this was NOT suggested by someone who was in possession of labia. Freddie was seventeen when he died, which makes a lot of sense when you look at his form. He very helpfully added a few diagrams of his own in the margins, and it was pretty clear that he hadn't seen many labia in the real world.

Still, I am not here to judge. My job is to simply go through the forms. Kidding!! OF COURSE I get to judge. This job would be super boring if I didn't.

I think Freddie is addressing a common theme Down There: how do you know if someone finds you sexually attractive? You really should know this, right? Especially if you are interested in seducing someone. I vaguely remember how that felt, though I was 108 when I finished my last life, so it wasn't something I was giving much thought to. Quite a few of the suggestions are about this, so we should sort it out. I suppose it's good that we have arrivals of all ages filling out the forms—gives us an overview of what is needed.

I've heard some men have uncontrollable erections (or they do at Freddie's age), so an uncontrollable labia clap is only fair. But we have to make it so that it can be controlled to some degree. What if a woman had a crush on her boss? Meetings would be really awkward. Or worse, her gynecologist—that would make exams unbearable (and maybe even impossible). So, I will put this one forward with the proviso that the

NOT CLAPPIN'
NOT HAPPENIN'

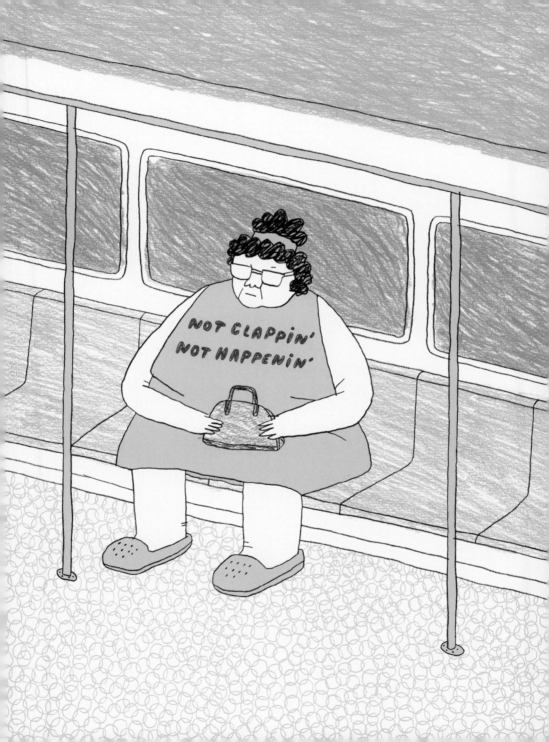

clapping can be stopped—maybe by crossing one's legs or pressing a small button behind the ears.

Side note: Good on Freddie for actually caring if a woman is interested before he approaches. If I see him in the cafeteria, I'll buy him lunch.

Back Scratching

NAME Helen O'Brien
CAUSE OF DEATH Tiramisu
SUBJECT OF UPGRADE Backs
REASON FOR UPGRADE That damn itch

UPGRADE SUGGESTION It should be easier to scratch your back so you don't need to use back scratchers, rulers, or your children.

In the original files on the human body, The Boss had written that "if a body part can feel an itch, it should be scratchable by the owner of that body," which makes total sense. But then there was a scribble in the margin of that page that I can't quite make out, but I think it says "bonding?????" (lots of question marks). I asked around and apparently The Boss decided it was good for people to be forced to ask for help with certain things. Seems He left a small area round the back that you can't reach yourself, so we aren't completely self-sufficient.

So rather than fix this one, maybe we should add some more things people can't do for themselves? As people aren't getting on as well as they could these days, they might benefit from a few more reasons to be nice to each other.

WARNING: Make sure we can still reach our mouths, noses, eyes, and nether regions, or it could get messy.

O*R*gasms

NAME Hayami Hada
CAUSE OF DEATH Landslide
SUBJECT OF UPGRADE Orgasms
REASON FOR UPGRADE Misplaced

UPGRADE SUGGESTION Orgasms shouldn't be the result of sex; they should be caused by reading. You finish a book—BOOM! That was incredible.

I am in favor of anything that makes orgasms easier and reading more popular. Would it matter what you were reading? Should there be a sliding scale? So, a self-published zombie apocalypse story gets you a slight twinge, while *War and Peace* results in an earth-shattering multiple big O extravaganza (now there's an incentive).

However, we would need a caveat that the orgasm has to be banked until you are alone. It would cause chaos otherwise. Schools and universities would be a nightmare—it doesn't bear thinking about. Commuter trains would be excruciating. Reading groups would have to go underground. Libraries! Imagine trying to keep the noise down with everyone reading furiously.

So now we only have procreation as an incentive for the sex act? It would curb population growth, the planet would be able to take a breather, and literacy rates would be through the roof.

Porn, sexual objectification, topless bars—all replaced by an obsession with reading, in a room of one's own. Writers would be the new sex gods. The *Times Book Review* would be the new *Hustler* magazine. George Orwell would be the new Channing Tatum.

And most of us know (but rarely admit) that lying by the pool with your favorite novel is usually more pleasurable than lying by the pool with your favorite pool boy.

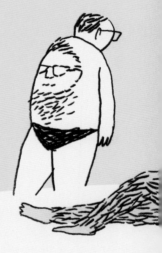

Back Hair

NAME Manuel Moreno
CAUSE OF DEATH Twitter pile-on
SUBJECT OF UPGRADE Back hair
REASON FOR UPGRADE Recognition

UPGRADE SUGGESTION Everyone should have back hair, but it should grow in the shape of your face, so that when you are walking away on the beach people know what you look like.

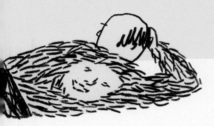

Everyone should have back hair, this says. That includes babies, and really old ladies in nursing homes, and sexy fashion models. It's important that we picture this when evaluating this suggestion, and not just think of Manuel, the lusty old Spanish guy who turned up at Check-In today in his Speedos (much to Gail's horror).

I would like to see some renderings of what back hair faces would look like, so I've asked for some drawings to be done. They are setting up a workshop between the guys from Hair and the guys from Backs, and the guys from Follicle Management. I've arranged sandwiches.

It's impossible to tell at this point how much value this would add. I'm pretty sure I'm going to shred this one, but if I head over to the workshop about an hour in, I will be able to pocket a couple of sandwiches. I've asked for extra cheese and pickle.

LUCKY ERECTIONS

NAME Jonny Chen
CAUSE OF DEATH Bungee jump!
SUBJECT OF UPGRADE Penis!
REASON FOR UPGRADE Fun!

UPGRADE SUGGESTION Some are winning erections that
tell you "Congratulations! This is your two-thousandth
erection!" And then you call a number and win some donuts!

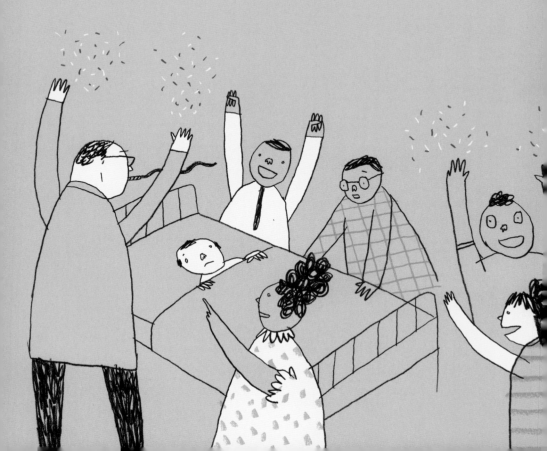

Easy on the exclamation marks, Jonny. You're exhausting me.

How would the message be sent? I've got a fortune cookie on my desk. ("You will experience great love"—yeah, right. I spend all day stuck in a box with two middle-aged admin obsessives.) Would something like that work? We'd have to look into where the paper would emerge. Maybe a tiny yet enthusiastic well-dressed man with incredibly white teeth pops out of the zipper and hands you a diploma. But imagine the litter.

Perhaps it's simply a voice like an intercom? I know The Boss has done a lot of work with disembodied voices, but historically they haven't been received well. Plus a strange voice would divert attention from the act at hand, so to speak. Imagine if Jonny had to memorize a number to call right when he was getting in the mood . . . Super annoying for his partner too having to fumble for a pen and pad of paper in the night stand. Forget it.

Also, this whole suggestion is very phallocentric. What about women—don't we like donuts?

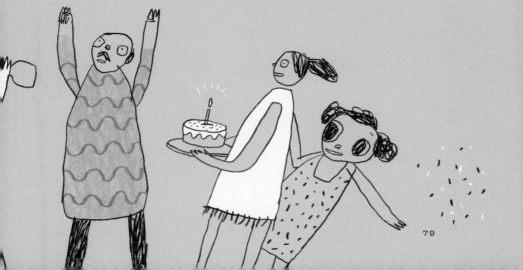

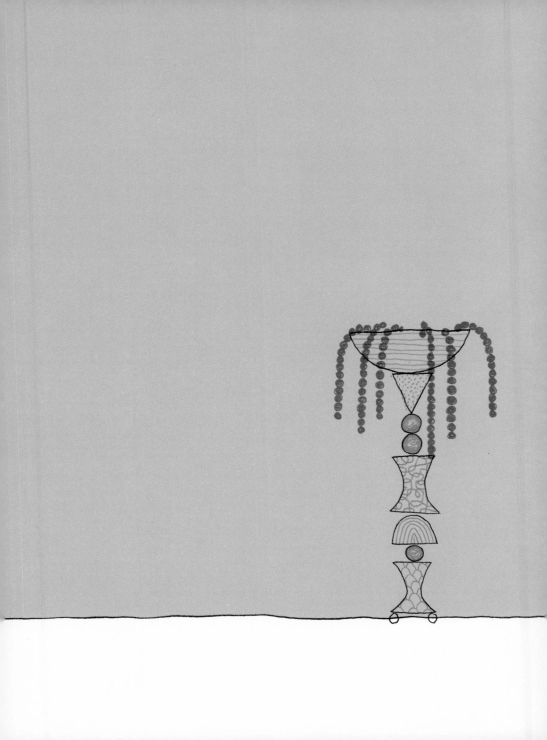

OH SHIT

Something really bad has happened.

I got called up to the third floor—I thought they were going to congratulate me on the extensive research I've done on bee enlargement. But there were four people (Gail, the head of HR, someone from Birds, and The Boss's PA) sitting in a row, and they all looked pretty ticked off.

It was about the flamingo changes I made last week. I filled out their leg width from half an inch to twelve inches, which clearly makes sense if you look at the poor things. It just didn't seem like something I should check with anyone, seeing as they were never officially approved in the first place.

Apparently, the flamingos flew to their feeding lakes as usual (so I got the aerodynamics right at least), but the increased leg mass displaced so much water, the lakes spilled over. Loads of villages have now flooded. Everyone's furious—some people have lost their homes, and their crops are going to fail. It's all my fault. They've had a Disaster Management Team on it all day.

I explained that I was "correcting" flamingos, rather than updating them, and told them about the "bring your child to work" day. The HR woman (who I think is on my side) said that does alter things, as she could see it more as me taking initiative rather than overstepping the mark. She suggested they look at it that way at least.

Even though the original flamingo was technically a mistake, it's always worked quite well, so their opinion was I shouldn't have tinkered with it. The other woman at the table seemed to be gunning for some kind of misconduct charge and really had it in for me. "What's next, elephants bouncing like kangaroos? NONSENSE!" Which, if I'm being truthful is quite a good idea, but I said nothing, stared down at my hands, and avoided all eye contact.

I've been suspended until Wednesday, when there will be an official review. Which means tomorrow I have to spend all day thinking about what an idiot I have been.

SUSPENSION

I forgot to switch my alarm off this morning, and I was halfway through brushing my teeth when I remembered that I had been suspended. I went back to bed for a bit and had a crazy dream where I was trying to run but my knees bent backwards, and then I looked down and my legs expanded until I was unable to move, and I was stuck in a school corridor and everyone was laughing at me and I blushed but instead of normal blushing I just turned bright pink everywhere—my hands, my body, and then I tried to speak but I couldn't open my beak.

When I woke up, I decided to pull myself together. If I've learned anything in my thousands of lives, it's that each moment is a gift, whether you are dead or alive. Or suspended. So I got dressed and went for a run in the park. Then I came back and sorted out my sock drawer and my hat collection. I cleaned out the fridge. I alphabetized my books and plucked my eyebrows. I tidied the kitchen cabinets, polished the cutlery, and cooked a stew for the week. I took out the recycling and brushed the floors. I filled in my gratitude journal, did some meditation, chanted my mantra, and did some yoga. When I finally felt ready to go to bed it was 4 a.m., and I barely managed three hours' sleep before having to wake up for the verdict.

WEDNESDAY

I was really nervous about my review—it was with the whole management team in one of those corner glass meeting rooms with a plant that no one ever waters. If I cried, everyone in this part of the office would see me. Maybe I had been a bit too eager to impress. Something like this was bound to happen eventually. I do feel bad about the floods, but no one could have predicted that. (OK, someone who was good at math probably could have predicted that.)

For the most part everyone was more friendly than I expected. The Boss was there, and He just crossed His arms and listened. The

HR woman said they investigated the "bring your child to work" day mix-up, and, big surprise, they found a few more birds drawn by the kids. Somehow the kids' drawings got mixed in with the actual bird designs, and they were put into production. They include the following:

- Peacocks
- Toucans
- Emus
- Pelicans
- And canaries, which surprised everyone. HR is going to look for the kid who did that one and offer them a full-time position. It is a classic design.

Now that they've sorted out the floods and crops, The Boss said we should all just move on. I like The Boss. He's obviously fair and reasonable, despite the loud ties and bright socks.

Overall, not as bad as I thought. The plan now: leave birds as they are, and check the other departments in case anything similar has happened. I wanted to say "maybe take a look at giraffes" but I thought it best to just keep quiet.

From now on, I'm just going to keep my head down and stay within the remit of the job.

OTHER KIDS' DRAWINGS

TESTICLES and Kidneys

NAME Tomas Schneider
CAUSE OF DEATH Wedding mishap
SUBJECT OF UPGRADE Body parts
REASON FOR UPGRADE Style

UPGRADE SUGGESTION Testicles should go back in, they're not pretty enough to be on the outside. Kidneys are a great design; they should be outside, and in a prominent position, so we can admire them.

Tomas was a furniture designer, which would explain this obsession with the aesthetic.

But he's not alone. We have had a lot of people complain about testicles—in fact, they were already under (slow) review when we started this project. It's come up time and time again in passing—at parties, for example. They are too wrinkly and saggy. Could they be a bit more smooth, like chestnuts, or cherries? Is the current design a waste of material? But nothing was ever done about it. It seems the penis gets all the attention, even Up Here.

But Tomas's suggestion would hide them from view, which would make a lot of people happy. When they were first designed, they had to stay outside the body to keep the sperm at the correct temperature, but Gail said the tech will have moved on by now, and it can't hurt to ask if there is a way of cooling things down while inside the body now. (Gail giggled a lot when she said it.)

On to kidneys. I agree, they are beautiful. Not sure if they could do their job if they were outside, however. They are quite delicate, and we can't risk damaging them. The best we can do is bring the testicles inside and give Tomas a job in Design.

Singers

NAME Franco Falcone
CAUSE OF DEATH Carpet burn (third-degree)
SUBJECT OF UPGRADE Singers
REASON FOR UPGRADE Confusion

UPGRADE SUGGESTION There should only be one singer allowed in the world at any given time. They sing all the songs until they die then another one is voted in. It takes too long to decide what to listen to, now we have all those streaming options.

I don't think I can agree with this. Musical taste is an important aspect of one's character. How will people know who to date? Or more importantly, who not to date? What if you were going out with someone who would be attempting to seduce you to their Hall & Oates playlist, for example, but you had no idea, because there IS no Hall & Oates?

We would miss out on one of the few chunks of information people are happy to volunteer at karaoke parties—like when Seamus sang that awful Spin Doctors' song at the Christmas do. I knew to turn him down when he asked me on a date.

There is a neatness that I like though. Maybe it's my OCD side. The idea of one musician who provides all the music to everyone in the world has its charm. We'd be able to focus on other, more important things. It's kind of like Einstein wearing the same clothing every day, which freed him up to invent physics or whatever it was that he did.

I just passed The Boss in the corridor on my way back from the snack machine, and He said "Hello Abby. Where are you flaminGOING for lunch?" and guffawed all the way back to His office. I laughed out of a combination of relief and surprise, not because it was funny. But it did cheer me up. He's such a dad.

Blushing

NAME Mirjana Novak

CAUSE OF DEATH Mushroom confusion

SUBJECT OF UPGRADE Blushing

REASON FOR UPGRADE It's just awful.

UPGRADE SUGGESTION When you are embarrassed, everyone else in the room goes red instead of you.

I remember blushing being useful when I was a young woman in England in the 1700s, because everyone thought me terribly coy and I had a fan to flutter in front of my face. But now it's just awkward. It certainly didn't help me when I was a news anchor, a few lives later, so I'd be happy to see the back of it.

I asked around if anyone would mind me getting rid of it, seeing as coyness isn't in vogue anymore. No one in the Shame, Guilt, or Flirting departments was able to give me positive feedback on blushing. The Head of Guilt suggested, "Get rid of it. Just make sure everyone knows it was your decision—I don't want it coming back on me." I got her to put that in writing.

But the feedback form suggests everyone else blushes, apart from the person feeling the embarrassment. That actually could be fun for a few years, and The Boss likes it when we show a bit of creativity. According to the Emotions department we can phase it out slowly, so I think we go with everyone else blushing for a few years, just to see what happens, and then get rid of blushing altogether.

I passed The Boss in the corridor again today. He said, "Hello Abby. Did you try the curry today? I thought it was a bit too FLAMINGo hot" and guffawed all the way back to His office. Again, I laughed, but He really shouldn't give up the day job.

LUNCH

Today some of the other interns asked me if I'd like to have lunch with them. We all met at Orientation but since then we've just passed each other occasionally in corridors. I usually eat my lunch with Tom and Gail, and the rest of the interns tend to eat together in the cafeteria, so it might be good to do something different for once. I worry that I'm missing out on some of the intern stuff (office gossip, happy hour invites, joining the foosball tournament), but then again my work is really important.

The cafeteria: Well, I can see why Tom and Gail bring their own lunch. Rows of tables and benches, with sticky ketchup, mustard, and mayonnaise dispensers (not even the good brands), and used trays everywhere. There is a fridge with sandwiches suffocating in plastic wrap, and a hot counter with the usual—crusty lasagna, some chicken thing, and a vegan carrot dish—everything seemed orange under the heat lamps. I got a small bowl, wiped the silverware on my shirt, and tried out the salad bar. I know how to work a salad bar—basically no leaves, just go for the high-density stuff: the beans, cheese, and a boiled egg.

We all sat at the interns' usual table. There are seven of them, all in their late teens (a popular age), and they've formed a bit of a gang. I think Jonty, who is working in Emotional Engineering, might have had a thing with Sabine, who does something in Weather. They were all talking about a party they went to the other night with some of the guys in Time (apparently the whole department turned up late the following morning with a hangover, and no one noticed that time hadn't been wound up until midday). It made me feel a bit left out, but there will be time for meaningless flings and gossip when I am back Down There.

Still, it was fun to be part of something for a bit, and they said they'll let me know next time they go out. I'm pretty sure Jonty winked at me when I got up, although some of the guys had just started a food fight, so he could have just gotten a pea in the eye.

FIXING FLAMINGOS

Nose Traffic Lights

NAME Maria Cotti
CAUSE OF DEATH Fisticuffs
SUBJECT OF UPGRADE Conversation
REASON FOR UPGRADE Dull people are unbearable.

UPGRADE SUGGESTION Noses could change color depending on whose turn it is to talk. Like traffic lights.

Nice one Maria. This could make conversations a lot less stressful. Or more stressful? Time to find out.

First we need to decide if the change happens automatically or manually. I need to speak to someone in Brains who can tell me if we can rig lights up to thoughts. Knowing how much people down there like to talk, I don't think we can rely on a speaker to give the green light to their audience fairly. I could be wrong, but I've seen enough political debates.

I would like the lights to change when the person's argument is starting to wane—maybe once they start leaving longer spaces between words, or they start saying phrases like "the thing is . . ." or "in my experience," or "but ALL lives matter."

Design-wise we have two options—a bulb on the tip of the nose, or inside the nasal cavity. I think we should go for the internal one to avoid changing the shape of the nose (we've only really started to get used to some of them). There is quite a lot of extra space at the end of nostrils that could accommodate a colored bulb. I've got Design on it now, and they will give us a working prototype by the end of the week.

I passed The Boss in the corridor on my way back from the restroom. He said, "Hello Abby, you sure you don't have a fever? You're looking a bit PINK" and guffawed all the way back to His office. I didn't laugh this time. It only encourages Him.

SPIDER WEBS

NAME Sakeasi Taukei
CAUSE OF DEATH Tap dancing
SUBJECT OF UPGRADE Spider webs
REASON FOR UPGRADE Too quiet

UPGRADE SUGGESTION Spider webs should be musical so when spiders walk around on them it sounds like they're playing a harp.

I am going to come clean: I HATE spiders. I'm sorry—I'm sure they're lovely people—but I really find them very unpleasant. So this is an interesting one for me. If I can get through this upgrade without having to see one, or look at photos of one, I will be happy. That's the best I can hope for.

Would a musical spider web make the whole eight-legs-making-thread-from-the-abdomen thing less disturbing? If you were a spider fan, I can imagine it would be quite comforting, lying there at night listening to the gentle *pling* (*plink? flonk? twing?*) of the spider harp.

Conversely, if I woke up to that I would be terrified. Although I would know what corner of the room to advance on while brandishing my slipper (or flamethrower).

While in some people a musical web would inspire a warm fuzzy feeling, in others it could inspire arachnicide (and would make it a lot easier to commit). We need to find out the spider's current approval rating Down There before we go for this one, because otherwise it's going to be spindly legged carnage.

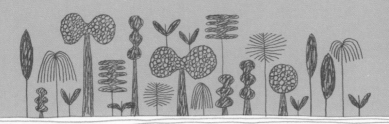

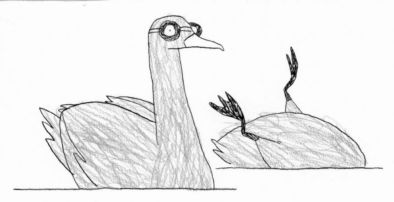

Swans

NAME Walter Stignac
CAUSE OF DEATH Golf riot
SUBJECT OF UPGRADE Swans
REASON FOR UPGRADE Perspective

UPGRADE SUGGESTION Swans should spend every other day upside down with their heads and necks under the water so they get the best of both worlds.

I wonder what made Walter care so much about swans and their experience of the world.

There are a few departments I have to contact for this one. They would have to be fitted with gills and a valve to stop them from drowning, so I need to speak to Aquatics. How would they propel themselves along if their feet were sticking up out of the water? Could their wings be deployed? That would give them a good amount of propulsion, so they'd probably be a lot faster on the days they were upside down.

What would they eat?

Would they need goggles?

They wouldn't inspire as many poems or paintings on their underwater days, but they might increase the amount of fish art, which is quite basic at the moment.

Basically, this one should be decided by the swans themselves. I would like to get a questionnaire out to the swan population in the next week or so. It's not for me, or Walter, to decide on their behalf.

Pigs

NAME Frank Gardino
CAUSE OF DEATH Idiocy
SUBJECT OF UPGRADE Pig stationery
REASON FOR UPGRADE Wrong

UPGRADE SUGGESTION Pig pens should actually be pig pencils because snouts are obviously erasers.

Frank, you are a moron, and I don't have time for this.

CaT SPoNGE

NAME Billy Diallo
CAUSE OF DEATH Genetic predisposition
SUBJECT OF UPGRADE Cat paw
REASON FOR UPGRADE Ease and efficiency

UPGRADE SUGGESTION One cat paw should be a sponge. Washing your whole body with your tongue must be hard work, especially if you're covered in hair. Pet owners could simply supply their cats with a small bucket of warm water and soap every morning.

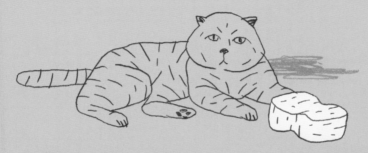

Billy arrived with nine cats in his luggage, which caused a lot of extra work for Gail as they weren't listed in her ledger. Cats are checked in somewhere else, so she had to arrange for a *tuk tuk* to pick them up and take them to be processed. They had to get a stamp from another department; it was hot; the cats got anxious; the batteries ran out on the *tuk tuk*. Gail finished off two packets of Oreos in quick succession.

I liked Billy. I only saw him briefly through Gail's hatch, but he was really smiley, and the cats were cute. Hopefully they can be housed together when everyone's paperwork is in order.

Back to the idea, which seems to be a good one. If one cat paw was a sponge and they had a little bucket, it would cut their cleaning time by at least half.

I put the application in to Felines and it was sent back immediately with the following note stapled to it:

"No. The extensive cleaning program is the only way we can keep them occupied. DENIED."

I've noticed that the Feline department is often very tetchy.

Giggling (TREES)

NAME Iliana Masi

CAUSE OF DEATH Banana peel

SUBJECT OF UPGRADE Tree laughter

REASON FOR UPGRADE Humor

UPGRADE SUGGESTION Could trees interact with us a bit more? Like giggle when you tell a joke or slap you on the back when you need a bit of encouragement? They don't really participate.

This one was a surprise. I made some good contacts when I was looking into leaf design, so I asked Farruh in the Tree department if he would like to have lunch. This is how to become successful here—eating overcooked spaghetti in the cafeteria with the people you need on your side.

Farruh told me that trees used to communicate a lot more with humans. Apparently, the Bible was full of conversations people had with trees, including a book written by a tree disciple. But it was scrapped because they were, as Farruh put it, "absolute bastards."

Apparently, trees have a cruel sense of humor. They laugh at any misfortune. They hate people and LOVE laughing at them. As a result, their ability to express their emotions in a way that humans understand was removed, so as to not upset anyone any more than they already had.

Farruh said trees ARE laughing, but we just don't see it. They have a complicated and sophisticated network of roots that allows them to take the piss out of us underground. He said that if we could hear them, we wouldn't even consider going for a walk in a forest.

Basically, by the time we'd started on the coffees, Farruh had convinced me that this one will have to be a no.

HEARING

NAME Nurlan Kadyrov
CAUSE OF DEATH Pardon?
SUBJECT OF UPGRADE Ears
REASON FOR UPGRADE I can't hear you???

UPGRADE SUGGESTION Hearing should get better and better with age, so you no longer have to wear an annoying hearing aid.

I don't want us to just reset hearing at a lower level, as it's useful in some of the early years, so we are talking about reaching abilities of hearing that currently are unavailable to the human ear. Is it gradual, or an upgrade that happens on your birthday?

Pros:
- No more shouting at old people (unless they're misbehaving).
- It would be nice to hear a ladybug walking over a blade of grass 150 feet away.
- It would be nice to hear your neighbors discussing how great you look for your age.

Cons:
- You'd need some peace and quiet sometimes.
- It would be awful to hear your neighbors discussing how bad you look for your age.

I am concerned that it would become incredibly intrusive, and humans would be forced to invent a "hearing blocker" which would end up being as cumbersome as a "hearing aid," and this will have solved NOTHING, Nurlan.

LEVITATION

NAME Marie Keller
CAUSE OF DEATH Fondue fight
SUBJECT OF UPGRADE Breathing
REASON FOR UPGRADE Curiosity

UPGRADE SUGGESTION When you breathe in fully, you should rise above the ground for a second.

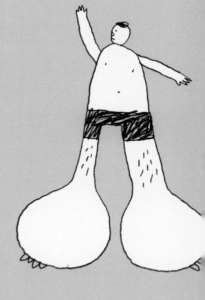

It's been ages since I greenlit a suggestion, and they're going to think I'm lazy. I'm going to say yes to this one, even before thinking it through. I know I don't have any real power (I haven't forgotten Flamingogate) but I am going to be quite enthusiastic with my recommendation as I send this upstairs.

The power went straight to my head. I wonder if Gail has any herbal tea.

I need to get Physics on the phone again, but they are a friendly bunch so I'm sure they can make this work. Tiny wings down the legs? Feet full of helium? An ass jetpack? People deserve to float once in a while—it's one of my favorite pastimes Up Here.

Internal Organs

NAME Dr. Jill Mahoney

CAUSE OF DEATH Ant farm riot

SUBJECT OF UPGRADE Inside

REASON FOR UPGRADE It's a mess in there!

UPGRADE SUGGESTION We need to reorder the internal organs—it's too crowded in there, and why do we need a football-field's worth of intestines, or whatever it is? Just a couple of organs with a tube joining them all, straight down. Job done!

I did pretty well in Biology in my last life, although I left school in 1931 and things may have moved on since then.

Let's say we get rid of all the unnecessary organs (spleen, hydrant, gall bladder, gasket, liver, pancreas, shower head) and shorten the intestines.

From memory, this is all we need for food and digestion: Mouth—stomach—intestines—butthole. One straight line, in and out.

And for the blood and oxygen stuff, we need: Mouth—lungs—heart—veins and things, er, heart—lungs again? Round and round?

UPDATE: The things you find out in this place! I spoke to someone from Organs in the mailroom today. Apparently, the reason we have such long intestines is that the manufacturer quoted fifteen feet per person for initial build in the early days—a complete rip-off! They are investigating, but the owner of the company has disappeared. If the revised design goes through, they will only need at most one foot of intestines per body, meaning we will have a surplus "intestine mountain." There's a meeting later to discuss what they could be repurposed for. Someone suggested potholes. The roads are pretty bad round here.

Body Vacuums

NAME Evgenia Mihailidou
CAUSE OF DEATH Fridge magnet avalanche
SUBJECT OF UPGRADE Cleanliness
REASON FOR UPGRADE Time-saving

UPGRADE SUGGESTION People should have tiny robot vacuums to clean their bodies when they go to bed.

Unfortunately, robot vacuums are patented, and it would cost The Boss millions to create a miniature one for human use.

How about if we just repurpose something that already exists? Like that little bird who stands on a rhino's back all day, eating parasites and flakes of skin and croissant crumbs (rhinos are OBSESSED with croissants). It would be great if we could employ a critter who has some downtime to take this on.

I'm not optimistic that anyone's going to apply, with all that sweat, body lotion, and unidentified gunk to deal with. Rhinos are surprisingly fragrant, compared to humans. I'll put something on the Jobs Board but I won't hold my breath (I'd advise the applicant to, however).

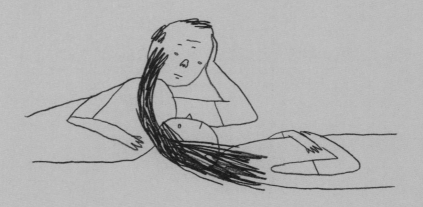

HaiR mOBiLiTy

NAME Dalibor Szabó
CAUSE OF DEATH Hot air balloon
SUBJECT OF UPGRADE Hair
REASON FOR UPGRADE Currently underutilized

UPGRADE SUGGESTION Hair should move. If I can wiggle my toes, I should be able to wiggle my hair.

I just sat here for ten minutes trying to imagine what it would be like to be able to move my hair, like a limb. Or a lot of limbs. Hundreds of thousands of limbs. If you had long hair you could reach over and stroke someone's face (or slap them). You could hug people with it. You could fight with it. You could fan it out in interesting shapes for a special night out. You could entwine it with the hair of loved ones. You could swim with it (imagine doing the back stroke with your arms AND your hair). You could curl and straighten it at will.

    We will have to look at the current musculature of the scalp and see if we have the capacity to add detailed movement to the follicles. I should really call someone in Nerves, too, but they're always so snappy. I think I will just send them a message and wait for them to get back to me.

Also, let's keep this head hair only. The last thing we need is pubic hair that can do things.

Shadows

NAME Dembe Nakyanzi
CAUSE OF DEATH Erosion
SUBJECT OF UPGRADE Shadows
REASON FOR UPGRADE Shyness

UPGRADE SUGGESTION Introverts should have the option to send their shadows to work on days when they don't want to engage with people. Shadows are underutilized. They could even be mobilized into some kind of army or employed in construction.

I never really thought about my shadow when I was Down There. What are they even for? They are useful if you're a vampire and you want to make a dramatic entrance into a candlelit room. They can protect a baby from direct sunlight if you've forgotten the parasol. They can make rabbit ears on the wall. You can't do much else with them, as Dembe has so rightly pointed out.

I requested some information on shadows and got this: "Shadows were initially intended to provide comfort and companionship to humans, and for a while this

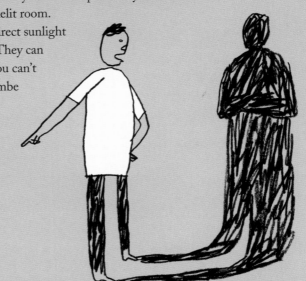

worked very well. Problems began, however, when the humans started noticing that the shadows disappeared at the end of every day, triggering their abandonment wounds. So they decided to stop talking to them to teach them a lesson. This in turn annoyed the shadows, who decided to stop talking too. We are stuck in a stalemate. Suggest mediation as this has been going on too long and everyone needs to grow up."

I will revisit Dembe's suggestion when the Legal department has managed to set up a meeting between representatives of the two parties.

Penis Colors

NAME James Magictorch
CAUSE OF DEATH Smiling
SUBJECT OF UPGRADE Male member
REASON FOR UPGRADE Brighten up the place

UPGRADE SUGGESTION Penises should be rainbow-colored, so the bigger the penis, the more colors it has. No one will brag about inches anymore; they'll brag that someone "goes all the way to violet."

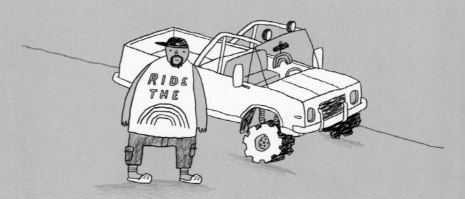

According to my calculations we can fit a small color cartridge (a bit like the ones we have for the expensive printer upstairs that no one is allowed to use) into the testicles. This will dye the penis as it grows—we're going with red, orange, yellow, green, blue, indigo, and violet. This will allow for James's hierarchy of color.

My only reservation is that James sounds like a bit of a knob.

Seashell Art

NAME Jen Bannister
CAUSE OF DEATH Shame
SUBJECT OF UPGRADE Taste
REASON FOR UPGRADE Lack of guidance

UPGRADE SUGGESTION Seashell art should be allowed to tell you off if you try to purchase it.

I am having to work on this while Gail is at lunch, because she loves seashell art. She has a shell seahorse on the wall above her desk, and a seashell-covered tissue box holder, and she has a seashell necklace that makes clacking noises when she gets up to make the coffee. If Jen's suggestion were to be implemented, she would have been subjected to quite a barrage of shell abuse over the years.

We don't want to make shells conscious. They'd likely clash with the creatures that live inside them (and you DON'T want to get into an argument with an oyster; I learned that the hard way). Plus they'd have to have a brain, a mouth, and language capacity, and we just don't have the budget for that right now.

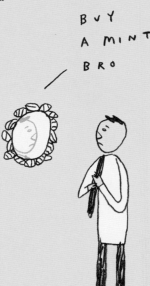

BUY A MINT BRO

We could do a motion-activated recorded message embedded in a chip in the shell membrane. We'll need a voice-over artist—someone said Cary Grant is still Up Here, and I reckon a British accent could work.

Suggested script:
You will never dust me; put me back.
No, I'd actually look tacky in the downstairs bathroom.
I will make all your outfits worse. All of them.
Is this really the image you want to convey?
Ooookaaay, Stevie Nicks!

It's a bit judgy, sure. Maybe seashell art is fine, and we should just let people be? (Jokes. This one is going through if I have to do it myself.)

Clearing

NAME Conchita Whirl
CAUSE OF DEATH Quicksand
SUBJECT OF UPGRADE Bathrooms
REASON FOR UPGRADE Community relations

UPGRADE SUGGESTION You should never clean your own bathroom. You should clean your neighbor's bathroom to encourage hygienic habits. Shame is a powerful motivator.

This is another one that would have to be added to Instincts—not that hard to do, but the implications have to be examined before we consider it. Instincts are powerful and often override our better judgement. I once had a passionate affair with a man who wore a white turtleneck sweater—my instinct to reproduce being stronger than my knowledge of right and wrong (thankfully I came to my senses before any lasting damage was done).

Conchita is right. Shame is a very powerful motivator. We could program this across the whole mammalian class. Cats burying each other's excrement, for example.

In the human family unit, babies could change each other's diapers—that could be useful.

Thoughts:
- What about people who live in remote areas?
- Royalty, celebrities, presidents? Confidentiality issues.
- What if you don't get on with your neighbor? It would be very hard to tidy their tampon boxes away efficiently if you hated them.
- What if you live next door to a burglar, or a murderer?

Thinking back to my last residence Down There, I lived next to a very unpleasant individual whose house smelled of cabbage. I wouldn't want to have to scrub their toilet bowl. Let's not do this, Conchita. Move on.

COUPLES

NAME Bunny Hopper

CAUSE OF DEATH Jumpsuit zipper

SUBJECT OF UPGRADE Romantic relationships

REASON FOR UPGRADE Verification

UPGRADE SUGGESTION All couples have to have sex with someone else on February 13 so they can be sure they are celebrating with the right person on Valentine's Day.

Hmmm. Who thinks Bunny just fancied a little action?

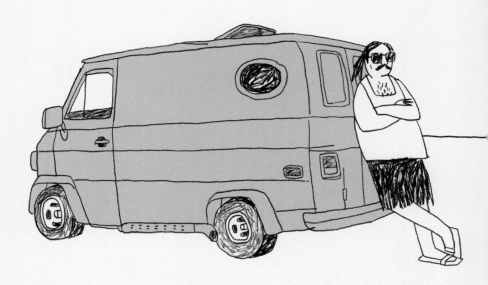

However, I have to approach each suggestion with an open mind. So, ignoring the fact that Valentine's Day isn't universal (and shouldn't be, what a waste of time, money, and energy it is), let's say February 13 becomes Sex With Another Person Day (we could call it SWAPD, or am I getting ahead of myself?).

We will have to get a saint to volunteer for this one, but they're all still Up Here so that won't be a problem. Plus, if I know saints, we won't have a hard time finding one to take this on.

I'm a little bothered by the wording ("have to") so we'll make this optional because, ew, Bunny. I'm also not sure what polyamorous utopia she was aiming for, but I'm pretty certain that a large proportion of couples who "opt in" would break up on Valentine's Day. Of course, the upside is not wasting time, money, or energy on Valentine's Day obligations. So there's something in this, but it's not good enough.

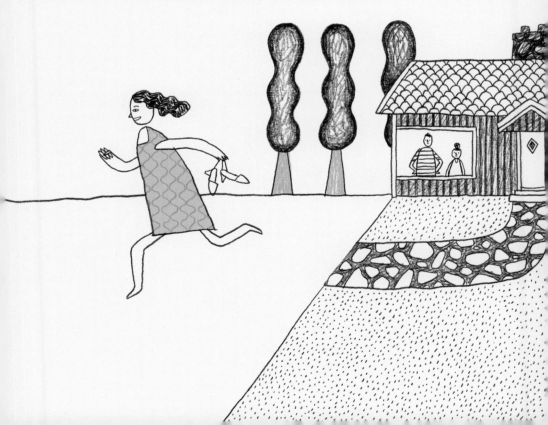

HAIRSTYLE SYNCHRONICITY

NAME Buck B. Tucker III
CAUSE OF DEATH American cheese
SUBJECT OF UPGRADE Hairstyles
REASON FOR UPGRADE Competition

UPGRADE SUGGESTION Hairstyles should synchronize, so if you meet your friends at 7 p.m., by midnight you'd all have the same hairstyle and therefore the same chance of scoring at the club.

This could have some benefits—take hairstyles out of the equation and maybe people would start considering the really important qualities when choosing a mate, such as kindness toward animals and health of bank balance.

But the idea requires a hierarchy of hairstyles—if Buck was in a bar with seven of his friends, and in a few hours they all had the same hairstyle, whose hairstyle would be the dominant one? Who has Alpha Hair?

Off the top of my head (yeah, I know), let's imagine Buck and his seven friends each have one of these:

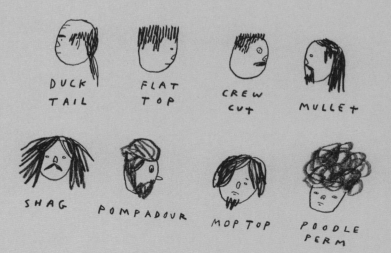

DUCK TAIL

FLAT TOP

CREW CUT

MULLET

SHAG

POMPADOUR

MOP TOP

POODLE PERM

Which hairstyle will they all have by midnight?

I need to find out if we could program the Alpha Hairstyle from a list like that one. Otherwise, how about we style some volunteers up here and put them all in a room and let the hairstyles fight for supremacy. I'd pay to watch that.

In fact, we've been asked to come up with entertainment ideas for the Christmas party, so it looks like we've found one.

BALL GAMES

NAME Billy-Bob Fledermaus
CAUSE OF DEATH *The Sound of Music*
SUBJECT OF UPGRADE Ball games
REASON FOR UPGRADE More exciting!!!

UPGRADE SUGGESTION In soccer, each player has a ball. Same with basketball. And volleyball! And water polo. And baseball. Shall I go on?

I love that Billy-Bob thinks we have any say in what happens in sport.

Rulers

NAME Barry Slipstream
CAUSE OF DEATH Biliousness
SUBJECT OF UPGRADE Rulers
REASON FOR UPGRADE Details are important.

UPGRADE SUGGESTION Someone should check that rulers are still the right length.

This isn't an upgrade, per se, but Barry is being helpful, and that's appreciated. While checking in, he also told Gail that her glasses were wonky, that she shouldn't wear her hair "like that," and that he got a splinter in his finger while resting his hand on the counter (a hand he'd used to steady himself after tripping over a stone left irresponsibly in the designated queuing area).

I sent a message to Measurements to check the length of rulers. And sure enough, they came back slightly out. They said there is nothing they can do about it without arousing suspicion, and that it's not really worth it anyway. "It basically means that if a guy tells you he's five foot ten on Tinder, and he turns up wearing Cuban heels, and you can STILL see his bald patch, he might not actually be lying."

As I write this, Barry is complaining very loudly about the lack of hand sanitizer available and asking if there are any antiseptic wipes for the pens.

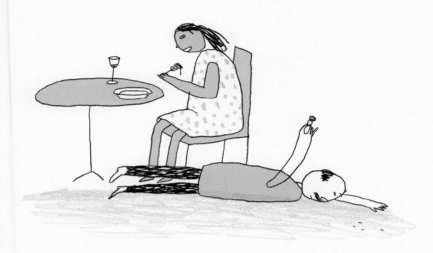

ProPosals

NAME Samuel Frink

CAUSE OF DEATH Conga collapse

SUBJECT OF UPGRADE Romance

REASON FOR UPGRADE More appropriate

UPGRADE SUGGESTION When someone proposes on one knee, the proposee should also get on one knee, forcing the proposer to lay on the floor in order to be lower down than the proposee. If the answer is no, the proposee should also lie down and they should stay there silently for about an hour, or until it stops being awkward.

I can't understand why Samuel wanted to change the traditional proposal style—the whole one knee/gasp/yes/tears thing we get in every rom-com. I quite like seeing men going down on one knee. You can almost believe, for just a moment, that they are chivalrous knights of yore, and they're not going to spend the rest of their lives scratching their balls, leaving their underpants on the floor, and staring vacantly into the refrigerator.

(I was married in a lot of my lives, and I've got to tell you, it was MUCH better being a husband than a wife.)

Let's have a look at this. We can change this—we just program a rewrite. Samuel's version replaces the one-knee version across the board— from Jane Austen to *Sex and the City* and all the versions of Cinderella. It will also replace everyone's memories, so grandma will "remember" how grandpa got chewing gum in his hair when he laid down during his proposal.

I'm going to see if Jonty (or one of the other interns, but hopefully Jonty) would try this out with me in the cafeteria later. Just to see what it looks like. Then I'll take a vote (it's taco day today, so it will be busy).

Swear Words

NAME Moonbeam O'Shea
CAUSE OF DEATH Undercooked frankfurter
SUBJECT OF UPGRADE Bad language
REASON FOR UPGRADE Vulgarity

UPGRADE SUGGESTION Swear words should be replaced by numbers, so you could shout "You're nothing but a 5-71-23, and my sister thinks so too!"

We need to assign numbers for each swear word, and I think it would be easy to get one of the more immature interns to volunteer for this. I found a Dictionary of Swear Words in the Library, but it dates from 1885 (I haven't heard "rantallion" for at least three lives).

Tom suggested we add a "My Favorite Swear Words Were: . . ." section on the feedback forms, and then update the dictionary at the same time. Two birds, one stone. I've put in a request with HR for another intern. (I'm thinking Buster, or Scrappy, or Kareem, or Findus, or any of the boys, really, apart from Jonty.) It will make them even more unbearable than they are already, but we all have to suffer for our art.

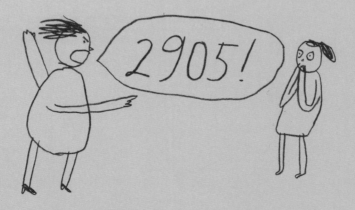

War

NAME Countess Angelelli
CAUSE OF DEATH Flat tire
SUBJECT OF UPGRADE War
REASON FOR UPGRADE What is it good for? Absolutely nothing.

UPGRADE SUGGESTION Wars should just be the leader of each country giving their opponent a good shove. The country who loses is the one whose leader falls over. It should be televised live so everyone knows the outcome.

If we go for this, humans will have come full circle. I remember in the very, very early days when we were living in caves (we were preverbal then, which had its good points), wars did mostly consist of shoving. And grunting. I shared a really

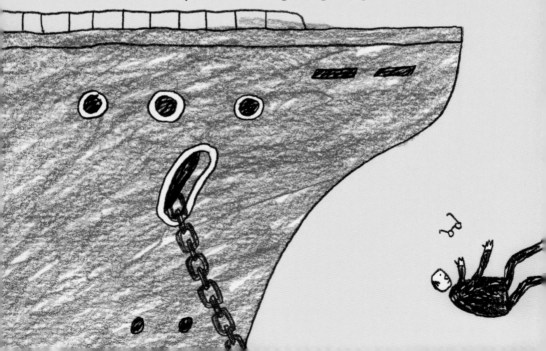

big cave with someone (he didn't have a name, but neither did I; we got by) who was excellent at shoving. You could say we rose up through society pretty swiftly and it was all down to his shoving abilities. Hands flat on the opponent's chest, a big strong push from the outset, very loud grunt at the same time, and terrible, terrible breath (amazing I still remember that, 3 million years on). Boy, was it effective.

Then cave disputes turned into small group rock-throwing, which turned into large-scale rock-throwing battles, then weapons got more sophisticated, and battles turned into wars, and more people got involved, and now we have millions dying, horrific injuries, devastated communities, refugees, and weekend war reenactment groups.

Let's go back to two people shoving. The Boss wanted the big questions sent straight to Him, but is this serious enough? War is serious. Shoving isn't serious. Which is the point of this suggestion, really.

I'll send it to Him.

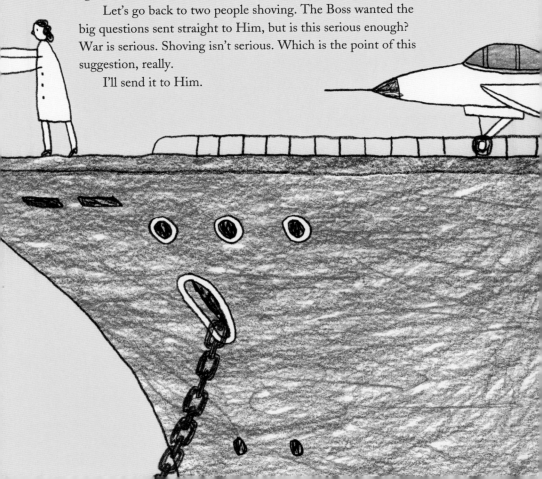

CEO Shrinkage

NAME Ahmad Hussain
CAUSE OF DEATH Dentist
SUBJECT OF UPGRADE Bosses
REASON FOR UPGRADE Character improvement

UPGRADE SUGGESTION If you become a boss, a CEO or a president, you automatically shrink one foot.

All successful business people would be tiny, which I can't say would be a bad thing. They would actually want to be the smallest in the room—so no more shoe lifts or excessively high heels.

Really successful CEOs would need high chairs at the dinner table, which would be hilarious.

Office furniture would get smaller and smaller the higher up the company you go. This could lead to a fairer redistribution of space. No more squeezing ten lowly employees into a tiny room while the head honcho has a space the size of a swimming pool, and all the good plants.

However, I fear The Boss, The Ultimate CEO, might have something to say about this one.

JOB INTERVIEWS

NAME Mimi Philippe
CAUSE OF DEATH Changing a duvet cover
SUBJECT OF UPGRADE Job interviews
REASON FOR UPGRADE Mood

UPGRADE SUGGESTION Job interviews can only take place when both participants are sufficiently drunk.

Not everyone drinks though, Mimi. This would be a disaster for non-drinkers, who would be overlooked in the employment market, and end up on the streets, begging for a few coins to buy a sparkling water.

Honestly, who makes the right choice when they are drunk? In the history of alcohol and history: NO ONE, which I suppose is the whole point of alcohol. Mimi sounds fun, but I have a suspicion she was virtually unemployable, and she should focus on that for a while.

Aggression

NAME Floella Burbage
CAUSE OF DEATH Zumba
SUBJECT OF UPGRADE Aggression
REASON FOR UPGRADE It's silly.

UPGRADE SUGGESTION When people get aggressive, they break wind. Just an embarrassing *parp*, not an offensive smell.

I read this feedback form just before lunch, then went to the cafeteria. There was a bit of a kerfuffle in the queue for the salad bar (something about someone taking the last of the croutons). There was some elbow jostling, and for one terrifying moment I thought the Caesar salad dressing jug might have been upended.

I was able to imagine in real time what this Feedback suggestion would look . . . er, sound like. An embarrassing *parp* would have ended the whole thing immediately. Aggressor would have been embarrassed, victim wouldn't have had to defend himself, and salad dressing would never have been endangered.

Emotional Engineering says that it will take a few days to sort out, but that they will test it on the salad bar queue later this week. Apparently, they do this kind of thing a lot, without telling us, which is probably a breach of our rights, but I'm not going to make a fuss as it's working in my favor. It also explains why there are never enough croutons.

Turtle Shells

NAME Eduard Giorgadze
CAUSE OF DEATH Rage
SUBJECT OF UPGRADE Shells
REASON FOR UPGRADE Unimaginative

UPGRADE SUGGESTION Turtle shells should have way more interesting shapes. They are so disappointing when compared to, say, the snail or the conch.

I asked Frank, a turtle, how he felt about this suggestion, and he was deeply hurt. He says that if you speak turtle, you understand that their shell shape is a convoluted declaration of their identity—something that grows with their character and tells other turtles important information about them. For example, the design elements on Frank's shell apparently tells other turtles that he is "easygoing, open to new experiences, and up for a laugh."

We obviously don't want to mess up turtle communication, but I think we could do something with color. Frank said he would like that, and he favors a pastel palette.

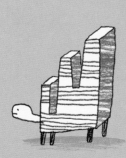

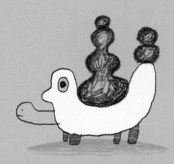

121

Eating Children

NAME Sigridur Gudrunsdottir
CAUSE OF DEATH Elves
SUBJECT OF UPGRADE Children
REASON FOR UPGRADE I have many reasons.

UPGRADE SUGGESTION Parents should be allowed to devour their children's friends if they don't find them suitable.

I have had many children over my lives, and I loved them, but that was mainly because of hormones. Children are much harder to love when you aren't flooded with oxytocin and under a biological imperative to keep them alive. This is why other people's children are unbearable.

This does worry me slightly. I didn't like any of my children's friends. And considering how many lives I've lived, under this rule I would have eaten hundreds of thousands of children.

Which is fine, but how do you make them palatable? Ketchup? Some of the larger kids would need a lot of sauce to get them down. Do we need child-size hot dog buns? Fried onions? Or do we make a big casserole once a week and just keep adding more kids and root vegetables?

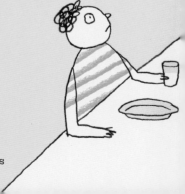

I've just realized that this would mean other parents would have eaten my children, and me at various points. (I was often a revolting child.) I'm not sure the human race would be able to continue. It would mean only the ones with no friends would survive, and that's looking scarily like our modern political landscape.

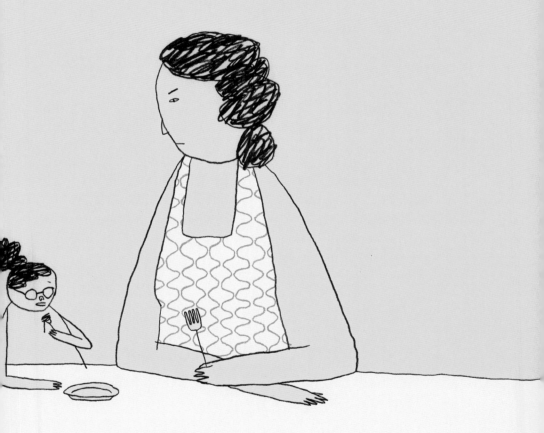

ANTS

NAME Barbara Vans
CAUSE OF DEATH Undone shoelaces
SUBJECT OF UPGRADE Ants
REASON FOR UPGRADE Useful transportation

UPGRADE SUGGESTION Ants should be able to be trained like horses, so we could ride a carpet of forty thousand ants to work, or to the local grocery store.

That does sound fun, and we know for a fact ants love working together on projects. Do they care if that project is building a new underground colony, or taking Barbara to Costco?

This could be a great solution to the fuel problem, as I know for a fact that Barbara drives that gas-guzzling old station wagon everywhere. If she had a carpet of ants to take her around, her carbon footprint would be reduced dramatically.

Cyril up in Insects said that this could work, but the ants would have to see Barbara as their queen, which means they'd feed her on a daily basis. From what I know of Barbara, that won't be a problem.

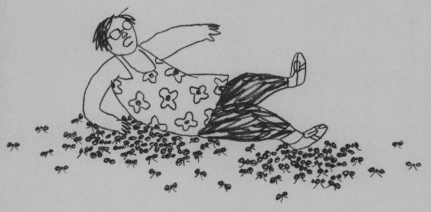

SNAKES

NAME Santa Santamaria
CAUSE OF DEATH Jell-O deficiency
SUBJECT OF UPGRADE Snakes
REASON FOR UPGRADE They're scary.

UPGRADE SUGGESTION Snakes should just roll around
sideways instead of slithering; it's less creepy.

I tried this out with a pencil on my desk. According to my calculations it
would reduce the "yikes factor" of snakes by 38 percent.

I organized a meeting with someone from Reptiles who turned out
to be a boa constrictor, which I wasn't expecting (thankfully I'd booked
the long meeting room). His only reservation was that snakes normally
live in jungles, with a density of trees. "If we have to roll around sideways,
we won't get very far." So the choice, according to him, is going with the
upgrade and moving snakes into a less cluttered landscape (plains, deserts,
interstate highways) or leaving things as they are.

I will set up a poll.

WORMS

NAME Ludmilla Andreu
CAUSE OF DEATH Bullfighting
SUBJECT OF UPGRADE Worms
REASON FOR UPGRADE Ease

UPGRADE SUGGESTION When worms eat dead bodies they
should expand and swallow them whole like pythons do, and
then lie there for a week until the whole body has been
digested. The mourning period is over when the worm has
returned to its normal size.

There is something very calming about this idea. I see it as going like this:

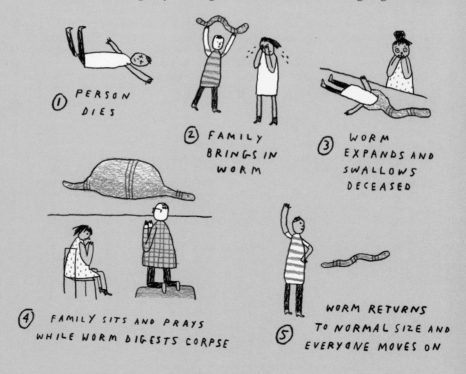

1. PERSON DIES

2. FAMILY BRINGS IN WORM

3. WORM EXPANDS AND SWALLOWS DECEASED

4. FAMILY SITS AND PRAYS WHILE WORM DIGESTS CORPSE

5. WORM RETURNS TO NORMAL SIZE AND EVERYONE MOVES ON

Funeral homes would have to adapt, but it would save a lot of cemetery space.

We'd have to ensure that worms don't "jump the gun" and start trying to devour people before they pass. The last thing they need Down There is an epidemic of killer worms.

GRAPES

NAME Fleur Magritte
CAUSE OF DEATH Men
SUBJECT OF UPGRADE Grapes
REASON FOR UPGRADE I'm tired of wine.

UPGRADE SUGGESTION Grapes should already be alcoholic so that you don't need to make and bottle wine. Hic!

Fleur was the owner of a well-known vineyard, and she died in her nineties, so it sounds like she'd had enough of the wine-making process. I can see how if she'd just had to pick the grapes and sell them, her life would have been much easier.

But grapes instead of wine? Toasting the bride and groom, for example, might seem less ceremonial if you just had to hold a grape aloft. And what percentage of alcohol is in each grape? If you only had to eat one to get tipsy, that would be pretty cool. If you had to eat several pounds before finding your date remotely attractive, it would ruin dinner. Plus you'd probably spend most of the evening on the toilet.

FIXING FLAMINGOS

One Animal

NAME Greta Weber
CAUSE OF DEATH Mint shower gel
SUBJECT OF UPGRADE Animals
REASON FOR UPGRADE It would be neat.

UPGRADE SUGGESTION Someone should mate all the animals in the world together—so a lion with a tiger results in a liger, the liger mates with a mule, and so on, until we end up with one super animal that can count every single animal in its ancestry.

I had to call a big meeting for this one—the sandwich order was massive—and we didn't get very far. There was a lot of shouting over what the One Animal would look like. The elephant guys were saying "it has to have a trunk" and the pig guys wanted to take the tail, but the beaver reps were furious about that and threatened to strike. The Fish department wanted to know if they were going to be involved at all, and birds—well, they've had enough to deal with recently.

The upshot was that the lab is going to do it "organically" and see what we end up with. If The Boss likes it, He will approve it. It's going to take a while so I probably won't be Up Here by the time it's decided, but I guess I may bump into it Down There in a future life (literally, if the Kangaroo Team have anything to do with it).

Squirrels

NAME Caleb Hammersmith
CAUSE OF DEATH Hula-Hooping
SUBJECT OF UPGRADE Squirrels
REASON FOR UPGRADE Employment

UPGRADE SUGGESTION Squirrels should be given jobs.
Besides gathering nuts, maybe they could pick up litter?

Job suggestions have to be run by HR, so I sent them an email, and they invited me to the office to "throw some ideas around." It was me, Neil from HR, and Shirley, who is the agent for squirrels. She kept asking me what would be in it for her clients, and that there was no way they would be picking up litter for free.

Apparently, they might be interested in adding "Minor Garbage Disposal and Recycling" to their remit, but they want twenty vacation days, an increase in nuts, and health insurance.

Fur

NAME Philomena Bennet
CAUSE OF DEATH Indignation
SUBJECT OF UPGRADE Fur
REASON FOR UPGRADE Cruelty

UPGRADE SUGGESTION All animals should wear fake fur. It's
disgusting they are still using real fur.

There has been some activism Up Here regarding this recently—a family of mink had red paint thrown at them, and someone protested a rabbit colony.

I'm going to suggest we add something about this to the New Arrivals Orientation program. Honestly, what are they teaching young people Down There these days?

Dragonflies

NAME Sybil Sassoon
CAUSE OF DEATH Cannoli
SUBJECT OF UPGRADE Dragonflies
REASON FOR UPGRADE Inappropriate naming

UPGRADE SUGGESTION Dragonflies should behave a bit more like dragons—where are the fire breathing and the damsel kidnapping?

Dragons aren't extinct, you know. They have retreated to the tops of the very highest mountains, where they try to get on with their lives as quietly as possible. They can't stand humans—not many species can, to be fair.

But not for the obvious reasons like war, pestilence, the destruction of ecosystems, and so on.

Dragons just can't stand the sound of people eating with their mouths open, chewing gum, cackling laughs that go on too long, sniffing (they really hate sniffing). Dragons are ultra-sensitive to this stuff. If they were on social media, they'd be calling themselves introverts and writing "oh god, that's SO ME" underneath articles about misophonia.

Dragonflies have an arrangement with dragons—they do all their shopping, pick up their meds from the pharmacy, pay their bills, and so on. We could add fire-breathing to their repertoire if it would keep Sybil happy, but I'm not sure it's really worth it.

Bigfoot

NAME Linda Kralova
CAUSE OF DEATH Waterslide
SUBJECT OF UPGRADE Bigfoot
REASON FOR UPGRADE I've never seen him.

UPGRADE SUGGESTION Bigfoot should be a bit more present, like Loch Ness or Rick Astley.

What a coincidence. There was a posting on the Jobs Board recently asking for people to apply for Bigfoot. It's a short-term contract, because a couple of sightings is all you need to get everyone excited. It used to be the ideal job Down There for someone who was just out of college. You'd take it for a summer, hide behind trees for a bit, lope about in front of a couple of hikers. Job done.

Come to think of it, the job ad was half concealed behind a flyer for lasagna night, so I will move it to a more prominent position, and this one might sort itself out.

GO
23
19

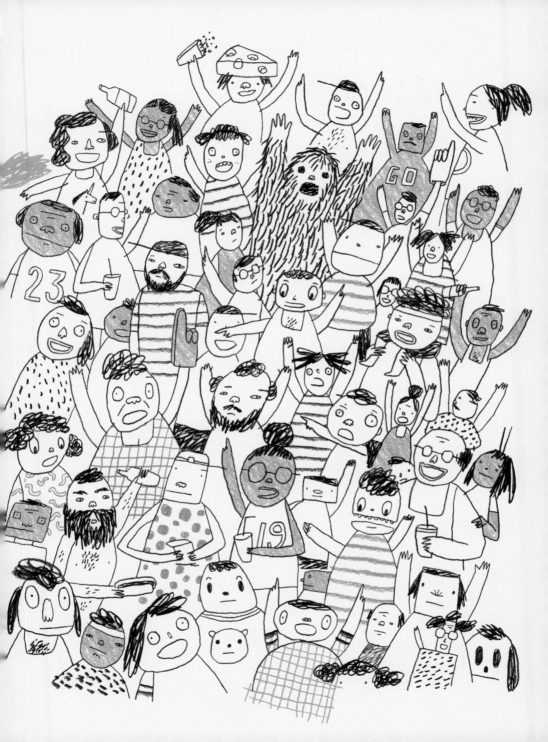

S_hEEP

NAME Beatriz Lopez
CAUSE OF DEATH Skateboarding
SUBJECT OF UPGRADE Sheep
REASON FOR UPGRADE Productivity

UPGRADE SUGGESTION Sheep should learn to knit jumpers using the wool they're wearing.

This is a very good way to make sheep more efficient. It is true that they don't do anything else while their wool is growing, apart from eating grass. (While we're on that—they never seem to get to a point where they've had enough grass. Have you ever seen a sheep look up, pat their belly, and go, "I'm full. Couldn't eat another blade?")

They will require hands in order to knit, as it's quite complex. You can't navigate knitting needles with those unwieldy hooves (or chopsticks, which I learned last week when I took a sheep to Mr. Wong's All You Can Eat Chinese Buffet).

We can replace the front two hooves of a sheep with human hands, but we would then need to make it possible for them to sit upright.

I did a straw poll with some sheep I know Up Here and they all said that would be great. Turns out it's really boring being a sheep. One of them asked if we could get them some jigsaw puzzles too, but we need to take this slowly. We don't want to overexcite them.

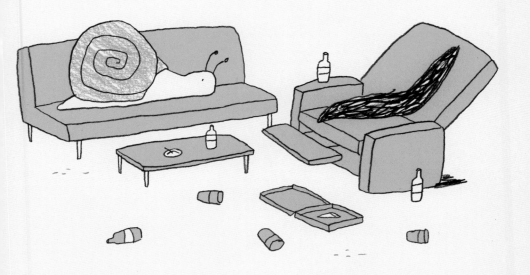

Snails and Slugs

NAME Mambo Nombafive
CAUSE OF DEATH Skirt length
SUBJECT OF UPGRADE Snails and slugs
REASON FOR UPGRADE Charity

UPGRADE SUGGESTION Snails should budge up and let slugs
live with them. The homeless gastropod situation is
appalling.

I put in a call to the Gastropod Guy (that's how he advertises himself on
late-night TV Up Here). He said: "Why should the hardworking mol-
lusks who managed to get on the housing ladder be forced to share with

losers who didn't pay attention in school? If we're not careful we'll end up like the commies" and just went on and on until I put the phone down.

I think the best option would be to look into setting up a better habitat for the homeless slugs so they're not always out there when it's raining, getting stepped on by toddlers or eaten by birds (or stepped on by birds and eaten by toddlers). I've put in a request to Ecosystems to see if they can ask one of the larger-leaved plants if they'd mind setting up a refuge.

Facial Hair

NAME Blaine Maindrain
CAUSE OF DEATH Flying saucer
SUBJECT OF UPGRADE Facial hair
REASON FOR UPGRADE Hunger

UPGRADE SUGGESTION Facial hair should be edible. But you can only eat your own, not other people's.

Blaine is onto something here, without knowing it. Apparently Santa has such a long beard because he spends so much time "on the road" and if he runs out of food, he has his beard as a reserve meal. I asked him what it tastes like when I met him at the Summer Party (he can never make the Xmas shindig). He said, "Have you ever tried rhubarb? Well, it's nothing like that. Kinda yeasty." That put me off the vol-au-vent I was holding.

I spoke to Fabrice in Hair and he said edible facial hair can be rolled out to the rest of the population if we want. It's pretty easy, although it does favor men as they have more of it. He said we could just make ALL hair edible, because even bald men can grow a beard. (I've asked if we can leave pubic hair out of it though, for reasons of dignity.) It's a good solution, so I'm sending this one upstairs for further evaluation.

FIXING FLAMINGOS

Pheromones

NAME Sally Ballpark
CAUSE OF DEATH Went berserk
SUBJECT OF UPGRADE Pheromones
REASON FOR UPGRADE Compatibility

UPGRADE SUGGESTION Pheromones that tell you whether your musical tastes are compatible.

I thought pheromones helped you identify someone whose immune system was a good match for yours, so you can have the best baby. But maybe musical taste is more important.

I asked Tom what he thought and he said, "My ex and I split up over which Cyrus was better—Billy-Ray or Miley"—but he answered the phone before I could find out which one he favored, and now I'm looking at him in a new light. I've never thought of him having exes before.

I went over to the Sexual Attraction department to find out how easy it would be, but I got distracted by the guy at reception, who was really hot. My mind went blank and I stammered something about dropping off a parcel, and came back to my desk.

I decided to phone instead, and finally got through to someone called Hank. He said we could add musical tastes to the Pheromone List, but we should talk about it over dinner some time, so I put the phone down.

I think an email would be safest. That, and a cold shower.

WEIGHT GAIN

NAME Lana Gisler
CAUSE OF DEATH Streetdance
SUBJECT OF UPGRADE Weight gain
REASON FOR UPGRADE Frustration

UPGRADE SUGGESTION You choose where you gain weight. So if you want a bigger butt, you could eat a huge cake and hey presto! Instant junk in the trunk!

I have some points, although I am mostly in favor of this:

- How would you tell your body where to gain the weight? I would definitely want a few rocky roads to go to my chest but my hips are already of reasonable heft.
- It would need to be reversible. I ate a lot of cake in my last life. I can't begin to imagine the size of MY junk (or trunk?) by the end of 108 years.
- Would it be immediate? Imagine if I went for afternoon tea somewhere swanky, and I was wearing a lovely pants suit, and the pants split halfway through (I can't control myself around cake; it's one of my few character defects). I'd need a few hours to get home and into my caftan before the weight gain appeared, or it could be really embarrassing (not embarrassing enough to turn me off cake, though).
- What about people with no access to butter, flour, eggs, and sugar?

ARMS

NAME Francis Flimflam
CAUSE OF DEATH Poisoned chalice
SUBJECT OF UPGRADE Arms
REASON FOR UPGRADE I like hugs.

UPGRADE SUGGESTION Are arms long enough? If they were double the length you could hug two people at the same time, or hug one person twice.

The following points need to be considered:
- Sleeve lengths—coats, sweaters, and shirts will all get a lot more expensive.
- Knuckle dragging—we left this behind a few million years ago. Do we really want to go back?
- Wristwatches will be further away from eyes.
- Pianists will have to sit way back from their pianos.

Will we be better at tennis, or worse? I can't work it out. I will get the Limbs Team to have a look.

MUSCLES

NAME Tom Aquino
CAUSE OF DEATH Dropsy
SUBJECT OF UPGRADE Muscles
REASON FOR UPGRADE Motivation

UPGRADE SUGGESTION Muscles should pump up in real time at the gym and last twenty-four hours, so you can be ripped for a date but fit better in a suit for a job interview.

The idea of being able to actually see the results of your exercise as you're doing it is brilliant. You could just work out until you were happy, go out into the world, and slowly deflate throughout the day. You could nip to the bathroom for a few push-ups if you wanted to up your game on a date, or be a bit more imposing in a meeting.

Someone in Muscles is "on it, baby" so we will get a report back soon.

WINDOWS

NAME Flavia Swank
CAUSE OF DEATH Jam addiction
SUBJECT OF UPGRADE Windows
REASON FOR UPGRADE Efficiency

UPGRADE SUGGESTION Windows should taste nice so we won't need window cleaners anymore.

Who says they don't already?

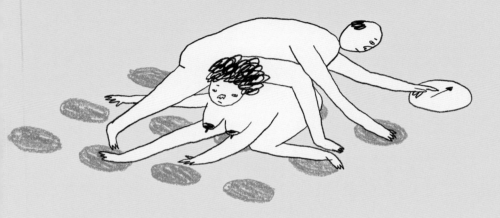

Erection Direction

NAME Levon Mephisto
CAUSE OF DEATH Trampolining
SUBJECT OF UPGRADE Erections
REASON FOR UPGRADE It would be kinda funny.

UPGRADE SUGGESTION Erections should randomly point in different directions, forcing you to be more creative with your sexual positions.

The Boss will LOVE this one. One of the things He's most proud of is how He managed to make the sexual act completely ridiculous, while still maintaining it as a driving force for humanity. He said He always has a "good giggle" when He watches people "getting it on" (and He is watching, believe me). I could bet my well-worn copy of the *Kama Sutra* that He will approve this update.

Flying

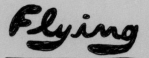

NAME Celestine Moncrieff

CAUSE OF DEATH Profiteroles

SUBJECT OF UPGRADE Flying

REASON FOR UPGRADE Incentives

UPGRADE SUGGESTION Some people should be allowed to fly.
Obviously not everyone, it would be chaos up there. But
maybe it could be earned.

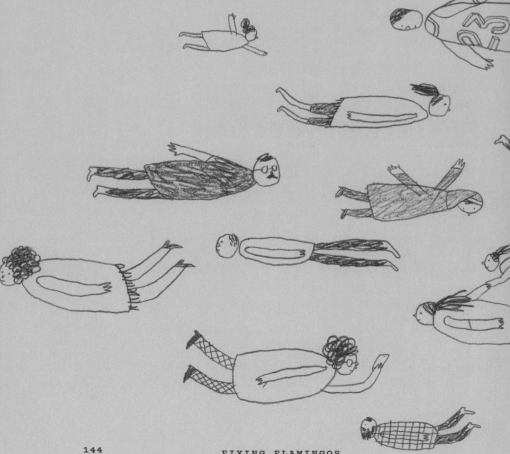

There is a page in our official handbook detailing why humans can't fly, because it's a question that comes up a lot when people arrive Up Here. The human ego is much bigger than it should be (which is what has caused most of the problems over the last few millennia) and some people are indignant that they weren't allowed to fly.

HANDBOOK, CHAPTER 11, PARAGRAPH 3: "Humans can't fly because not everything has to be about them. Birds can't do macrame, for example, but they're not constantly asking me about that. Accept it and move on."

Celestine's idea of flying being something people could earn is interesting, however, and I think it's worth putting to The Boss. We've had a few reward schemes, but no one seems interested in becoming a saint or being revered as a prophet anymore.

Something like this might be considered:

- Tending to the sick and needy (one month) = four hours of flying
- Feeding the hungry (two months) = six hours of flying
- Texting politely after a date, even if you don't want to see them again = fourteen hours of flying
- Dancing in a summer camp and being falsely implicated in a pregnancy scandal and then returning and doing some more dancing and not putting Baby in the Corner = twenty-five hours of flying.

He does like an incentive scheme, so I'll send this one up to Him. It's that or vouchers.

Anger

NAME Flyover McBride
CAUSE OF DEATH Rice cakes
SUBJECT OF UPGRADE Anger
REASON FOR UPGRADE Peace, man

UPGRADE SUGGESTION Anger should be replaced with itching. The angrier you get, the itchier you get. You'd do everything in your power to calm down and work out a peaceful solution. And calamine lotion would be illegal.

Brilliant idea. I called my contact in Nerves again and described the suggestion over the phone (but only once they'd stopped shouting at me for calling instead of sending an email. So tetchy.) I was allowed to describe this suggestion. All it needs, apparently, is a rewiring of the nervous system. Easy enough! We booked a nerve engineer to work out the circuitry and they should have a prototype by next week.

Everyone's pretty excited about this. We even came up with a name for the prototype: Mr. Giggles. We'll probably do some early tests with Mr. Giggles in an angry situation—say flicking it repeatedly on the ear or forcing it to stand in the queue at the cafeteria when there are only a few portions of quiche left. I'll suggest Mr. Giggles spend a day in our office when it's Gail's turn to choose the radio station.

Knees

NAME Jake Bhura
CAUSE OF DEATH Rock climbing
SUBJECT OF UPGRADE Knees
REASON FOR UPGRADE Need a redesign

UPGRADE SUGGESTION Knees should be better designed. You should be able to bend forward and backward on them, or even swivel in all directions. Kind of like an owl's head.

I've asked for the original blueprints of knees to be sent over so I can have a look. Turns out one of the original engineers is Up Here for a bit, and she's offered to sit down with me over a coffee.

Update: Lori, the knees woman, came over and we went through the possibilities. She said she's quite excited about doing a redesign. So were chair designers, and Cirque du Soleil acrobats, who sent a nice email in support (subject line: Think of the possibilities!).

Lori explained (although this is a secret) that at one point The Boss was considering getting rid of knees altogether, and just having people walk around with two long stick-type things with no bend in them at all. He had been alarmed at the amount of knee surgery people were having Down There and thought maybe this would sort it out (plus His PT kept getting Him to do lunges, and He really hates lunges).

It was a chance meeting at the Xmas party that stopped Him: He was doing the twist and one of the leg guys mentioned how involved the knees are in almost every dance. The Boss loves dancing. When the leg guy explained that dancing without knees was virtually impossible, He said that whoever came up with the idea of getting rid of knees was an idiot.

Lori will give me some new swiveling knees to try out next week.

Double Chins

NAME Donna Winter
CAUSE OF DEATH Parkour
SUBJECT OF UPGRADE Chins (double)
REASON FOR UPGRADE They're not that bad.

UPGRADE SUGGESTION Can we make double chins attractive? They're pretty much inevitable once you hit middle age, so why can't we just enjoy them?

Donna makes a good point here: double chins are very hard to avoid without surgery, once you hit a certain age. Men can always grow a strategic beard, but often the wobble gives it away. Turtlenecks should be fine, but just aren't, which is one of life's great mysteries. We could bring back the Elizabethan ruff—I had a spectacular one in one of my lives, but I did get a lot of crumbs stuck in it.

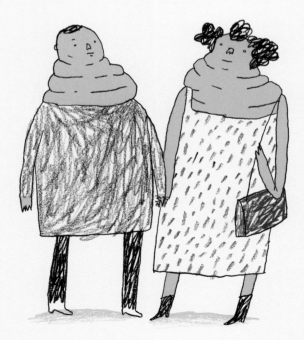

The main problem with making them sexy is that some people are inevitably going to overdo it. There will be bigger and bigger chins, and chin implants, and pretty soon everyone will be walking around like a bunch of tree frogs on mating night. It's actually making me feel a bit sick just thinking about it.

NiPPLES

NAME Jerry Vermouth
CAUSE OF DEATH Hot wash cycle
SUBJECT OF UPGRADE Nipples
REASON FOR UPGRADE Ease

UPGRADE SUGGESTION Nipples should actually be solar-powered lamps, so you can read your book at night. You'd simply charge them in the sunlight for a few hours each day.

Women's nipples already have a pretty important function, Jerry. I'm not sure if you noticed?

We'd have to have a security latch in place so they don't accidentally dazzle a baby mid-feed. Otherwise, this is a pretty good idea, as no one really knows what to do with men's nipples, and they would look lovely lit up, nestled like Xmas lights among the chest hair.

I'm going to pretend I don't think Jerry is a bit of a creep who just wants to ogle tits all day long, simply because this is a good idea. Have you ever stayed in someone's spare room and realized that there was no lamp on the bedside table? You read your book until you get sleepy, only to wake yourself up again when you have to cross the room to the light switch. Fuck that. Solar-powered nipple lamps are a great answer to this problem.

INTERN LUNCH DATE

This morning I was going through the forms trying to find an interesting one to get my teeth into (I don't think anyone cares, as long as I get them all done. Which will never happen as the pile just gets higher and higher). There was a "ding"—I'd not heard it before, so I looked around the room just before Tom said, "Check your computer." And there it was. Jonty (the intern from Emotional Engineering) had sent me a message. Our interoffice-intranet-internal webanet system (or whatever it's called) is so unreliable, most people don't use it. But here was a message. I clicked Open.

"Hi Abby. Fancy lunch today? I heard there's shepherd's pie. Meet at the cafeteria at 1?"

I left it thirty minutes before I replied. I didn't want to seem too eager, but I was quite excited because he's definitely the hottest intern Up Here.

"Hey, that would be great. See you there." (I spent ten more minutes deciding whether to end the message with an exclamation mark, but as you can see I went without it.)

Then I decided to talk myself out of being excited. Especially as Jonty seems to have worked his way through most of the female intern population (or so I've heard).

Still, I checked my hair before I left, because it's very important to look smart and presentable at all times, in case I bump into The Boss in the corridor again, for example.

Jonty was sitting at a table near the window when I arrived, and he waved me over. He'd already got us two servings of shepherd's pie, which I thought was kind of romantic but also hugely arrogant. I was torn really between the audacity of him acting like someone in a 1940s movie, and the fact that I really wanted shepherd's pie. So I decided to leave it, and just tuck in.

We did the whole small talk thing, which I always find excruciating. (How are you, how's the job going, did you hear about bla bla bla, are you coming to the party, oh I'm sure they meant to invite you, the mashed potato is good, and so on.)

He told me a little about Emotional Engineering and the work they do there. Emotions need to be assigned to each experience in order for humans to make the most of their time. As the list of experiences available to humans grows, each one needs to be assigned a number of relevant emotions. For example, when stage-diving became a thing in the 1970s, the Emotional Engineering Team had to tag a number of emotions to the experience—in this case fear, hysteria, joy, shame, and regret.

He said his team sometimes messes around with the emotional tags—last week they swapped the emotions for skateboarding (excitement, euphoria, terror) with emotions for origami (peace, tranquility, contentment). They left it that way for a couple of hours but swapped them back when alarms went off—a load of skateboarders in London ended up in the ER, and an old people's home in Kyoto reported a breakout: "Sixty-five elderly people escaped, like baby turtles running for the sea."

Then he asked about what we are doing on the Updates Team. I told him it was just me but I'm only working on smaller stuff (I tried to be humble)—insects, animals, some minor physical alterations, but I get to work on my own and mostly get to do what I want. I mean, that's the great thing about this job—while The Boss is busy sorting out the big pressing issues of life (you've got to have the greatest mind working on pandemics and bigotry, for example), I'm quietly handling the smaller things.

Jonty put down his fork and looked me in the eyes, which made my tummy feel a bit funny and my face start to flush. "But you're changing the world, Abby. They might be small changes, but that doesn't mean they're insignificant. You must be really good for them to trust you this much."

I didn't want to tell him about the flamingo fuckup, so I just looked down and said something about the shepherd's pie. But now I'm back at my desk, and I can't stop thinking about it.

This IS important work. I AM changing the world. And Jonty looks like Ryan Gosling.

COLLAPSIBLE SKELETONS

NAME Jenny Handstands
CAUSE OF DEATH Champagne cork
SUBJECT OF UPGRADE Skeletons
REASON FOR UPGRADE Flexibility

UPGRADE SUGGESTION Humans should have collapsible skeletons like mice, so we could slide under doors. We'd lose our shoes though.

The Mouse Skeleton Team was happy to come and talk to the Human Skeleton Team, as long as we provided refreshments. I took the orders. There are A LOT of people on the Mouse Skeleton Team—about three times as many as on the Human Skeleton Team. This may explain why mice have the updated Collapsible Mk7 Skel-E-ton, and humans are still on the practically immobile and constantly degrading Skellington Version 1.1.

They did a lot of drawings and made some little models out of matches and adhesive putty. They ate forty-seven cheese sandwiches, thirty-six mini pork pies, and eight large pizzas. If The Boss wants to go ahead with this, the majority of the Mouse Skeleton Team will move over to Human Skeletons for a while, leaving a skeleton staff of only three over on Mouse.

I am not sure whether this would be a good update, however. Crime is bad enough in the human population. This would effectively make it easier for them to burgle each other, yet harder for them to incarcerate each other when they get caught.

The Mouse Team said mouse crime didn't rise much when they added this functionality. I'm unconvinced—we've all seen *Tom and Jerry*.

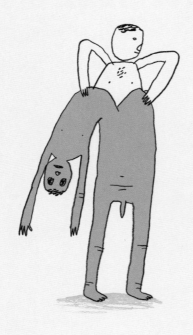
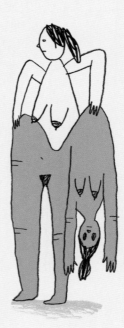

Shedding Skin

NAME Fable Neoprine

CAUSE OF DEATH Plagiarism

SUBJECT OF UPGRADE Skin

REASON FOR UPGRADE Youthfulness

UPGRADE SUGGESTION Humans should shed their skin, like snakes do. It would save money on expensive skin care.

How often would shedding take place? Once a month would be fun—around payday? Then you'd really look forward to going out, flashing the cash, and the youthful complexion.

I asked a passing snake how it feels, and he said, "Very itchy for a day or two, and you just wriggle around until it all starts to loosen. Then you just pull yourself out of it." Apparently, we need to think "less pantyhose, more wetsuit."

The Boss will have to decide whether this would mean humans never age. I am against this idea: aging teaches you humility, which is something we could do with more of Down There. Plus, they've got Instagram filters now. But I can imagine it would feel nice to "start again" every month. Like having a really good bath.

We are trying to be more sustainable these days, so I suggest this only gets approved if the skin can be recycled into something useful. A few of us discussed this over lunch (coincidentally, no one finished their sausages).

Top 3 Skin Uses:
- Food: Apparently, it contains valuable nutrients. You could eat your own skin while it sheds, and then there would be no mess. If you were in love you could eat each other's skin. If you were rich (or full) you could donate your skin to a food bank.
- Mattresses: Pile all your skins on top of each other and sleep on them.
- Wet weather clothing: Skin is waterproof, right? I'm thinking boots, capes, umbrellas, tents?

Baby Hair

NAME Dinka Claptrap
CAUSE OF DEATH Gout
SUBJECT OF UPGRADE Babies
REASON FOR UPGRADE Do I need a reason?

UPGRADE SUGGESTION Babies' hair should take after the color and hairstyle the mother had the night she conceived.

This one is more complicated than it looks. We need the egg to be aware of the woman's hairstyle, so the genes can reassemble once conception has taken place. If remembering the hairstyle was left up to the sperm, it would never happen. You can't get sperm to think of anything but the goal, at that point (or any other point, to be fair).

We need a communication channel from brain to egg when she starts the mating procedure, something like "bouffant, auburn with blonde streaks, perm growing out, shoulder length," which would then get coded into the genome. If conception is unsuccessful at that point, it resets to [blank] and then starts again next time the antics start up again.

Then the baby is eventually born, with a great hairstyle (hopefully). The parents are reminded of the night in question ("oh, it was the night you tried parting it on the left"). It's kind of pointless, but then, isn't everything?

Armpits

NAME Monty Fripp
CAUSE OF DEATH Luge accident
SUBJECT OF UPGRADE Armpits
REASON FOR UPGRADE Lunch

UPGRADE SUGGESTION Armpits should be hot enough to keep your lunch warm while you're at work.

Two things need to be done here. First we need to increase the available space in an armpit to safely hold a burger, mug of soup, or leftover curry.

Secondly, we need to adjust the temperature. Currently, armpit temperature ranges from around ninety-seven to ninety-nine degrees. Soup is best at around 150 degrees.

The Boss has gone very eco-friendly these days, and I know He's going to want a modern heating solution. Something that uses a process that is normally taking place when people are at work. How about boredom—the more bored you are at work, the hotter your armpits?

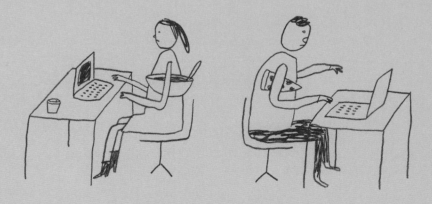

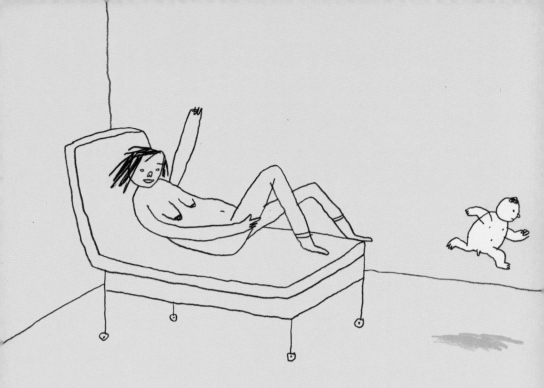

Babies Running

NAME Phylicia Boobies
CAUSE OF DEATH Had enough
SUBJECT OF UPGRADE Newborn babies
REASON FOR UPGRADE Safety

UPGRADE SUGGESTION Babies should be able to run when born. Like gazelle or deer. That way the wolves won't get them.

Phylicia isn't messing about here—for a baby to outrun a wolf, we are talking FAST.

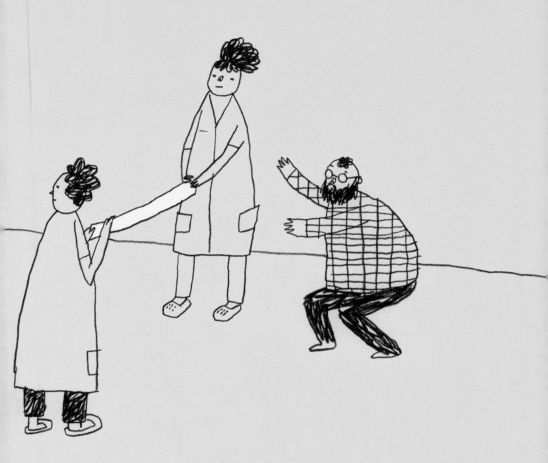

Pros:
Babies could run out of the womb, saving on labor cramps and push-ing. The midwife could just wait at the end of the room with a towel and some orange segments.

Cons:
Looking after toddlers is hard enough. Imagine having to look after a newborn who could run a sub–four-minute mile.

There was a message on the Jobs Board this morning: "Looking for a hip young web surfer who knows how to get the likes! Help set up our social media presence. Interns only. Lunch is included. Must have previous Down There social media experience." Then there were little dangly bits of paper off the bottom with a fax number for HR. The fact that we even have a Jobs Board with bits of paper pinned to it says so much about what an uphill struggle this is going to be. Also: a fax number . . .

Teenagers

NAME Minty Binliner
CAUSE OF DEATH Hairspray
SUBJECT OF UPGRADE Teenagers
REASON FOR UPGRADE They're awful.

UPGRADE SUGGESTION Humans enter a "cocoon phase" between the ages of thirteen and nineteen, as long as their parents have ample space in the garage.

Minty is right: Teenagers are awful. I conducted a poll using one hundred of today's check-ins—ninety-eight said teenagers were, indeed, awful; the other two were dogs, who love everyone, so they don't count. I decided to discuss this with the Insect department, so I arranged a call (I'm not going in that creepy building). They said it would be best if the teenager starts making their own cocoon on their thirteenth birthday by spinning a web-like substance from their midriff (they can repurpose the belly button for this). It would take a couple of days to completely cover a regular-size thirteen-year-old. When the child is completely cocooned, the parents (hopefully managing to hide their glee) take them to a cool, dark space (cellar, garage, attic, church hall) and suspend them from the ceiling.

They would need to be fed occasionally—my contact said a few large Cokes per week poured into their feeding hole (or mouth) would do the job.

Then they emerge on their twentieth birthday. The parents eat the cocoon (and THIS is why I don't like the Insects crowd; they're always adding caveats like this). The young adult moves out and gets a job. Parenting is over.

Hairy Feet

NAME Bobbolo L'Amour
CAUSE OF DEATH Pak choi
SUBJECT OF UPGRADE Hairy feet
REASON FOR UPGRADE Warmth

UPGRADE SUGGESTION Hair should grow on the bottom of your feet to keep you warm.

Toward the end of my last life, when I was in my nineties, I discovered those fleece-lined, Velcro-flapped slipper booties that old people wear. I became obsessed and had to get them in every color (Sage, Blush, Visiting Hour, and Heather). I remember thinking how unfair it was that the feet are so vulnerable to the cold. They are often so far away from the rest of you. A thick layer of hair on the bottom of the feet would be a life-saver for people who can't afford the booties. And if you lived in warmer climes, you could just shave.

I'm calling the Hair guys all the time these days, but here goes.

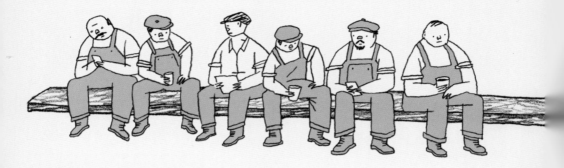

Jameses

NAME Franz Gripp

CAUSE OF DEATH Silliness

SUBJECT OF UPGRADE Jameses

REASON FOR UPGRADE I have my reasons.

UPGRADE SUGGESTION There should be some giant people called James who are eighty feet tall and who do all the manual labor.

OK Franz, weirdly specific, but I appreciate the extra detail.

I'm concerned this will cancel itself out. If we make 10 percent of the population eighty feet tall so they can do all the construction work, they will have to be solely employed in constructing houses, schools, universities, and building equipment for people who are eighty feet tall—at least for a few generations.

Someone who is good at math will have to come up with the exact figures, but I predict it would take about one hundred years for the

Jameses to assimilate into society, with their own infrastructures and communities and clothing across the world.

Initial Concerns:

1. What if some normal-size people enjoy building things? They might not want to retrain as dental nurses or geography teachers.
2. What if there is a war? I'm getting David v. Goliath vibes.
3. What if a non-James falls in love with a James? Will it become the new love that dare not speak its name? I thought we were getting over all that nonsense.

Naming them all James is another issue. Maybe some feel like Barry, or Pepita. And it could get really confusing on building sites: "James! Pass me the grappling hook!" "Not you, James, the other James, in the hard hat. No, the other James in the big pants, no . . ." and so on. Maybe James could be their surname. And what about regular-size Jameses? They'd be the brunt of all the giant jokes.

I'm not judgy, but this is dumb. Based on the sativa T-shirt Franz was sporting on arrival, I'm guessing this is more about the state he was in when he checked in, than it is about populating the earth with giants to do the heavy lifting. Franz had scrawled another suggestion beneath "Jameses." It just said: "Where can I get snacks round here?"

POTATOES

NAME Saira Patel
CAUSE OF DEATH Body boarding
SUBJECT OF UPGRADE Potatoes
REASON FOR UPGRADE Fashion

UPGRADE SUGGESTION Potatoes should be a better color—beige is unflattering.

It's funny, I could never wear beige (or camel, or fawn, or stone, or any of the other shades that are just beige in disguise), in any of my lives. No matter what skin tone or hair color I had, for some reason beige just didn't work on me. Maybe it just doesn't suit my soul.

So I'm all for this. I'm going to put a request in—neon potatoes would be amazing. Imagine the French fries.

KANGAROOS

NAME Dick Angevin
CAUSE OF DEATH Sweating
SUBJECT OF UPGRADE Kangaroos
REASON FOR UPGRADE I dunno.

UPGRADE SUGGESTION Kangaroos should no longer be allowed to jump. They should just have to walk around on their giant clown feet.

I wonder what happened to Dick to cause him to have such animosity toward kangaroos.

These upgrades are supposed to make life better for everyone involved, and I don't see who would benefit from this. No Dick. Let it go.

FIXING FLAMINGOS

Snoring / Purring

NAME Stacey Smom
CAUSE OF DEATH Forgot to stay alive
SUBJECT OF UPGRADE Electricity
REASON FOR UPGRADE Clean energy source

UPGRADE SUGGESTION Snoring (humans) and purring (cats) should create electricity.

Brilliant! We've been looking for a new energy source for a while. It would mean that people would have to sleep more, and cats would have to be kept constantly happy for societies to be successful. (I am going to put in a caveat that the snoring and the purring have to be done together, just because.)

Power stations will be replaced by giant beds covered in cats. People will be called up, a bit like jury duty (but with more cats. Note—get more cats into jury duty).

Henry over in the Energy department said it's totally doable—we just have to find a noninvasive way to hook participants up to the grid. In one night, an overweight middle-aged man with sinus problems could power a small office for a day (one room, three computers, a kettle, and a black-and-white printer). In four hours a very happy cat could create enough electricity to cook a three-course meal (soup, roast chicken, apple pie) and maybe have some left over to charge your cell phone.

It's little ideas like this that make my job worthwhile.

CHEWING NOISES

NAME Gautam Anthony
CAUSE OF DEATH Irritation
SUBJECT OF UPGRADE Chewing noises
REASON FOR UPGRADE What do you think?

UPGRADE SUGGESTION Please revise eating noises, they're unbearable. I've had over eighty years of this shit. Can't you make them cute, or funny? Like a dog's chew toy, I don't know.

I think we all agree with Gautam here, so I doubt this will be hard to get approved. In fact, I passed the form over to Tom during lunch while Gail was eating her mung bean stew, and he gave me a very enthusiastic thumbs-up. Poor Tom—they've been sharing this tiny office for many, many years.

There is a Department of Icky Noises that handles all the—well, it's self-explanatory really. I have been advised to send over a list of sounds that could replace the Traditional Eating Squelch and they will do some testing. I've come up with a rudimentary list:
- Dog's chew toy (as per Gautam's suggestion)
- Harp (lovely)
- Comedy bike horn (funny)
- A voice saying "yum yum yum yum" (topical)
- Waves crashing/whale songs (peaceful)
- A medley of Madonna's early singles (maybe not the one where she makes all the sex noises)
- Horse's hooves on a Victorian cobbled street (quaint option for holiday dinners)
- Machine-gun fire (edgy option for teenagers)
- Fireworks (maybe blinking lights could be involved)
- An owl (I'd go for this one)

I have asked if we can set our own eating noise, like a ringtone on our cell phone. People could personalize them. I have a feeling this is going to end up being more annoying than the Squelch, in the long run, but there's only one way to find out. Note: Gail loves "Material Girl." I hope Tom does too.

Noses

NAME Jean-Claude Vanaret
CAUSE OF DEATH Passion
SUBJECT OF UPGRADE Noses
REASON FOR UPGRADE Uncomfortable

UPGRADE SUGGESTION Noses should flatten when you kiss so you can do it head on. It would save space when kissing in confined spaces such as voting booths and wardrobes.

This is a problem, and, of course, it took a Frenchman to point it out. Also, how embarrassing is it when you lean in and both tilt your head the same way? And then you laugh and both tilt your head the other way. Then you finally make contact but cringe all the way through the first kiss.

I've drawn up a rudimentary model with a retractable nose—following the same design as a theatrical stunt knife, where the shaft disappears into the handle.

With my new design, lovers can approach a kiss as if they were about to do a very slow headbutt (emphasis on slow here, people). As their noses make contact, they retract into a new cavity in the head. (I've removed a bit of brain to fit it all in, but no one will notice.) This will allow kissers to stare directly into each other's eyes, if they don't find it too creepy.

Then as they pull apart, the noses return to their original position.

Potential Problems:
- The hinge mechanism gets loose, and noses retract every time the head moves
- Some of the larger nose designs might have to be taken out of circulation
- Boxing? Cocaine? May impact some lifestyles
- Squeaking

ExTENDABLE FiNgERS

NAME Luke Famalam
CAUSE OF DEATH Juice fast
SUBJECT OF UPGRADE Fingers
REASON FOR UPGRADE Emphasis

UPGRADE SUGGESTION Can we have extendable fingers for pointing? This would benefit teachers, coaches, and grandmas—the people who really should be listened to.

This could be effective but it needs to be controlled. If everyone had an extendable finger, it would become worthless. If, as Luke suggests, an extendable finger would benefit teachers, it should be denied to the students, or the classroom would end up looking like a game of pick-up sticks.

I've sent an email to the Digit department to ask how this could be incorporated into the current finger design. I've also requested a couple of extension speeds for different situations. If you're trying to make a point at the dinner table, a slow, steady extension would be useful. If you're trying to stop your wayward teenage daughter getting into a truck with her deadbeat boyfriend on carnival night, a quick draw would be advantageous.

Update: I've had a working model attached to the right index finger of Sammy, one of the interns who is at a loose end at the moment. I've asked him to spend a week employing the extendable finger where he feels necessary. What he doesn't know is that I've also sent a multi-departmental message asking people to report back to me if they see him using it. I have a feeling the extendable finger could be put to bad use, and attaching it to a socially awkward young man is the best way to find out what exactly those bad uses could be.

VERTEBRAE

NAME Harrison Squint
CAUSE OF DEATH Stopped living
SUBJECT OF UPGRADE Vertebrae
REASON FOR UPGRADE Shrinking is pointless.

UPGRADE SUGGESTION How about the ability to add extra vertebrae to the spine as you age? They could be topped up as needed.

When someone small checks in, Gail has to get up off her chair to peer down out of her hatch. You always know about it because she makes a lot of noise as she heaves herself onto her feet. She says it's important to give everyone her signature "welcoming smile" to make them feel safe (when she first did it to me I thought she was having a seizure, and called for help).

Harrison was one of the small people who warranted the heaving. I checked his file—he was nearly six feet tall at age twenty, but had reduced to five foot three by the time he arrived Up Here. The Boss said He added the shrinking feature so people could try different heights through-out their time Down There. But people have complained that they have enough to deal with as they get older.

Questions for Design:

1. Will vertebrae also be removable?
2. Where will they get the extra vertebrae from? We can't add a distribution facility this late in the game.
3. One size fits all? Unisex?
4. Painful?
5. We'll need a limit on the number of vertebrae someone could add, otherwise we could run into problems with torso arrangement. And doorways and ceiling lamps.

Saliva

NAME Tim Cinnamon
CAUSE OF DEATH Reggae
SUBJECT OF UPGRADE Saliva
REASON FOR UPGRADE Interpersonal relationships

UPGRADE SUGGESTION Saliva should change color depending on how you're feeling, like a mood ring. If you struggle to pick up visual cues you could just ask someone to open their mouth, or spit in your hand.

Saliva is handled by the Bodily Fluids Team. One of the team members, Sandy, was in the ladies' room this morning (she asked me to help zip up her hazmat suit). We got chatting. She said to give her a list of useful emotions and corresponding colors, run it by Emotional Engineering, and then she will review it.

I'm annoyed that I have to come up with the emotions. I guess everyone thinks this kind of thing is beneath them. In fact, I'm not annoyed. I'm angry. Sometimes I just wish I had a proper, established position, like Sandy in her hazmat suit.

Jeez, without me nothing would get done.

- Annoyance: yellow
- Anger: red
- Jealousy: green (obviously)

I'm going to get a coffee.

OK, I've had a bit of time to think about this. My job is actually pretty great. I'm given all this freedom to figure things out and be creative. It's kind of like building a second life, in real life, from the afterlife. Plus, everyone's been incredibly kind to me, especially considering I'm new to all of this. Sandy just caught me in a bad mood.

- Gratitude: blue
- Appreciation: lilac
- Regret: beige

In fact, thinking about all this made me cry. Gail noticed and passed me one of her homemade protein balls (they're disgusting, but it cheered me up).

- Love: pink
- Relaxation: peach

And then Jonty popped in to invite us all to a party next week (but he was staring straight at me), and that threw me again.

- Passion: purple

What the hell am I going to wear?

- Stress: orange

Body Fat

NAME Linda Tits
CAUSE OF DEATH Box-set binge
SUBJECT OF UPGRADE Body fat
REASON FOR UPGRADE Vanity

UPGRADE SUGGESTION Excess body fat should melt in the heat, allowing you to drain it off. You could have special channels on the beach to collect it. Maybe the fat could be used for something in manufacturing.

I'm glad Linda says "excess fat" here because otherwise living somewhere hotter than Linda's hometown of Oslo could be very dangerous. We need some fat or sitting down would be painful. Plus, warmth, sexy wobbly bits, Queen songs about body parts—all depend on fat.

I will get an official minimum body fat percentage from upstairs, and then people can drain as much as they want up to that point. You can't let people decide these things for themselves—look at their hairstyles, for The Boss's sake.

We also need to designate a drainage point on the body. It could seep through all the pores, but it might be uncomfortable, especially on a beach, to be covered in suntan lotion, melted human fat, and then sand. I'm going to suggest a spout in the lower back. Give it a few twists, and then gravity could drain the fat toward the hole. Sit upright to drain the upper body, raise the legs to drain the lower body.

Idea: If humans could convert drained body fat into fuel, they could at least offset their flights to their chosen holiday/fat drainage destination.

Saw Sammy in the cafeteria today. He said he's loving the extendable finger and will have a report ready for me as soon as he works out how to type with it. Then he whispered (ominously) that he's discovered some unexpected uses for it. I'm not sure I want to know.

He also told me that the social media internship has gone to a woman called Fran. She's older than they were hoping (forty-three) but it seems none of the younger ones would touch it. Apparently, she really raised awareness of feline HIV during the seven months she was Social Media Manager of a cat charity Down There and died with over thirteen hundred followers (three of whom went to her funeral).

SPRiNgy SKELETON

NAME Leonid Wincyette
CAUSE OF DEATH Thoughtlessness
SUBJECT OF UPGRADE Skeletons
REASON FOR UPGRADE Safer?

UPGRADE SUGGESTION Skeletons should be springy because too many people break bones falling over. Also, it would make parkour much more fun.

I went through the archive—it's still on microfiche, which makes me feel like a detective in a 1970s crime drama. A few thousand years ago they trialed a bone-mix formula of 50 percent rubber, for that very reason, but it was discontinued because (according to the file) "it is impossible to take anyone seriously [when they are] that boingy."

The file continues: "We found that the springier the limbs, the more humans laugh at each other. Essential activities such as territorial disputes and sexual reproduction are in danger of dying out very quickly due to giggling. Humans are facing a 'complete and abrupt species extinction event.'"

According to the file, they took the rubber out of the bone mix and early humans returned to fighting and shagging again.

I'll pass this up to The Boss in case He's looking for an upbeat way to remove humans from the game for a while. He still feels bad about how He handled dinosaurs.

Lying / Being Mean

NAME Plum Tiggerworthy
CAUSE OF DEATH Skipping rope
SUBJECT OF UPGRADE Lying
REASON FOR UPGRADE Justice

UPGRADE SUGGESTION Lying or being mean should have the same effect as smoking. It should take a few years off your life.

This is one of the fundamental mistakes people make when they're Down There. It's sweet that they think being alive is such a hoot. But once you get through Orientation you realize Up Here is where the fun really starts, and then you start wishing all your loved ones would hurry up and die.

The thing is, there are very old people still living who have been hideously mean and lied throughout their lives (war criminals, entertainment moguls—all moguls, come to think of it). Staying Down There is their punishment. They just go on and on, getting older and more uncomfortable, because being alive while being constantly horrible is really very unpleasant indeed.

(This doesn't mean that there aren't some great old people persevering with the life thing too. They're just the ones you have to call a cab for at parties.)

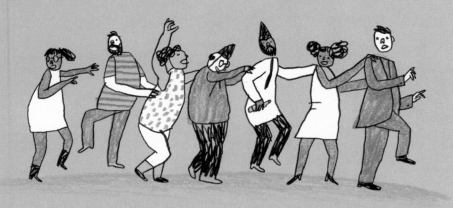

PARTY TIME

I was surprised that Gail and Tom wanted to come to an intern party. They're both pretty middle-aged, and in my experience, once you crest that hill, you're heading down to Boretown. In most of my lives I stopped wanting to party at about thirty-five years old. According to the Handbook, there are some traits that stay with you throughout ALL your lives, and that's one of mine—turning down the party invitations as soon as I can plead an age-related excuse. It didn't really cause much comment when I was a nun, but I was the most boring Roman emperor. They used to call me Yawnius behind my back.

Another of my repeat traits is punctuality. Even before the invention of the clock, I was always on time. Thrift is one of mine too—I once made broth for sixty-seven Mongol horsemen out of a piece of inde-terminate animal hide and a handful of barley, and everyone said it was delicious. Or rather, they didn't die. (Not from the soup anyway.) But the repeat trait I'm most proud of is focus. I am pretty single-minded once I decide to do something, which comes in very useful during my military lives. And this job.

And romance. Which brings us back to the party. And Jonty, of course.

It was being held in the sports hall, and it was to say goodbye to Findus, who has decided to apply for another life. He was interning in Hair. (I really hope my repeated requests didn't influence his decision to head back Down There.) Goodbye parties are always cool, because the person leaving finds out who they're going to be next. There's a New Life Reveal, where you open the gold envelope that contains the details of your life (nothing too detailed; they don't want to spoil the surprise). Then there's cake and drinks and dancing.

Gail was clearly excited. She said, "If it wasn't for you, no one would have thought to invite us oldies," and she ruffled my hair in a sweet and only slightly annoying way. Tom said we should leave work half an hour early, and Gail booked a blow-dry. We decided we would meet at the hair salon at 6 p.m. to pick her up, and all go to the party together.

I spent a bit longer than usual getting ready, while trying not to get too worked up over Jonty. He's really a bit too good-looking to be acceptable (or safe). Falling in love Down There is complicated enough, but Up Here it's a nightmare. It's impossible to make plans, or commitments, when things are so transient, so everyone tries to keep things light. If you catch feelings Up Here, you'll want to start applying for assignments Down There together. The New Life guys struggle to place couples together and are really bad-tempered about it, and it gets in the way of experiencing every aspect of life on offer. Plus, everyone Up Here takes a pretty dim view of couples—you stop getting invites to dinner parties, and people roll their eyes if you start writing poetry and sighing and staring into the distance.

The Boss always says, "You get enough drama Down There—don't you want some time off?" Solid point. Of course, He's a confirmed bachelor. I guess when you love everything and everyone, from the most insignificant microorganism in the bottom of the ocean, to Dolly Parton, to sand, and moss, and even all the politicians (I know, it's hard to fathom), it's impossible to choose one to love above all others.

I decided to wear the blue caftan with the feathers, my yellow bowler hat, the green rubber boots, and some white lace gloves ("Like a Virgin" was my favorite Madonna era). I'm known Up Here for my style (I'm beginning to think this could be another repeat trait, come to think of it) and I didn't want to disappoint anyone.

I headed down to the salon at 6 p.m. Tom was already there, waiting outside. He was smoking a cigarette, which I've never seen him do before, but otherwise he looked exactly as he normally does: the jeans, the fleece, and the shoes he always wears. I think he'd combed his hair though, and he smelled of either aftershave or window cleaner—I'm not sure which.

The salon door opened, and Gail came out with a head that was at least three sizes bigger than when she went in. Her hair had been crimped and teased beyond recognition, and she was wearing something very flimsy and sequined. I'm not sure if it was a bodystocking or a dress because it felt rude to look for too long. She had a glint in her eye that I have to say could be construed as sexy, if you were in that frame of mind. She was very giggly and said she'd had two glasses of wine already, "but it was that cheap shit so it doesn't count." Gail pre-gaming! I've never heard her swear before. The hairdresser seemed really glad to be locking up.

Gail hugged Tom and me way too hard and we set off to the sports hall, arm in arm, which was awkward as everyone was out of step. But at least Gail was upright, because in those shoes it was practically impossible.

The party was in full swing when we got there—say what you want about interns, but we know how to have a good time. A group of boys I recognized from Skeletons was throwing Findus in the air by the gym mats (safety first). Some of the girls who I've seen over at Perception were pouring something into the punch bowl. Sabine from Weather, who I thought had a thing with Jonty, was in the corner snogging someone who most definitely wasn't Jonty (phew).

Gail grabbed a beaker of punch, chugged it in one, refilled it, and set off after one of the lads from Digits. I turned round to raise my eyebrows at Tom, but he had started a conga and was leading the Emotional Engineering crew around the edge of the hall. I was beginning to feel like a bit of a lemon when I felt arms around my waist. It was Jonty, looking very dashing in knickerbockers, waistcoat, and ankle boots, and holding two beakers of punch.

He said, "Let's dance," and I was hoping we were going to do something sexy, like the rhumba or the merengue, but he pulled me out to join the conga, and we snaked around the sports hall tripping over folding chairs and plastic cups like a messy centipede. Then the gong went announcing it was time for the New Life Reveal.

Findus took his place on the podium and an official from New Lives handed him his envelope. Jonty had to shout for everyone to be quiet, because it was very rowdy by this point, thanks to whatever those girls did to the punch. Gail reappeared with lipstick smudged across her face, with the young man from Digits holding her hand and snuggling into her neck. Tom was playing shuffleboard with Sammy, who was denying cheating with his extendable finger.

Findus opened his envelope. "Lotu, a girl from a small village in Tonga!" Everyone cheered and the New Life official reappeared pushing a trolley covered in piles of Tongan dumplings in coconut sauce. They like to give you something to acclimatize you to your new surroundings when they can.

Jonty turned to me and said, "Shall we get out of here?" Of course, I said yes. We walked down to the cloud lake, which does this funny cotton candy thing in the starlight. It was looking particularly bouncy, and the sky-fish were leaping and making that joyful squeak they make when the vibes are just as they like them.

And finally, out there in the soft evening air, he kissed me.

It was a bit awkward, because when his lips met mine—and they are truly beautiful lips—I just thought how much better it would have been if we had those retractable noses. What if ALL the suggestions I've been working on these last few weeks had kicked in, especially the romance ones! He got a bit handsy, and I wondered whether swiping him away with my hair would be easier than with my hands. He mumbled, "What's up, baby" into my neck, which just seemed like the most awful cliche. "Can you HEAR me clapping?!" I snapped. And that was that. I picked up my cape and left, leaving him staring after me with a bewildered look on his silly gorgeous face.

It was only when I got home that it crossed my mind that I might be a bit too obsessed with my job. Actually, scrap that. I'm just the right amount obsessed with my job. It's the best job I've ever had, and I've had 4,325 of the fuckers.

THE DAY AFTER

People often drink too much Up Here because they can't believe hang-overs could possibly exist in the "good" afterlife. How wrong they are. Gail has been suffering all morning. Her hair is lopsided but thankfully she has managed to change her clothes since last night. She'd eaten her lunch by 10 a.m., plus the whole cookie stash, as well as Tom's half-eaten burrito from yesterday.

There's a suspicious-looking mark on her neck that MUST have something to do with Phil, the guy from Digits who she was dragging around behind her all night. He has called six times already, and each time she got us to pretend she isn't here. I feel for him. He sounds like he's got it bad.

I have to hand it to Gail. She's the ultimate professional, soldiering on through the hangover and managing to somehow be as kind, reassur-ing, and empathetic today as she normally is. I have a newfound respect for her. She knows that everyone checking in feels a bit lost. She's even had a few jokes with some of the guys who look like they're no stranger to a hangover. (The Hell's Angels chapter that arrived together after a mass brawl had such a laugh with Gail that they were late to Orientation and almost got struck off the intake list.)

Every now and again she crouches down underneath her desk with her head in her hands, groans, then takes a deep breath, and reemerges at her hatch with a welcoming smile. Incredible. What a trooper.

Tom has just offered to go to the cafeteria and get her some more food.

I'm not sure what to do about Jonty. I have really gone off him. It must have been the thrill of the chase. I am hoping the feeling is mutual as I haven't heard from him yet today. Fingers crossed he's moved on to someone else.

Well, that was wishful thinking. A bunch of flowers just arrived. First Gail thought they were for her and reached up to get her vase out, but Tom passed the card to me: "Thinking of you, Jxx."

I should have known this would happen. Jonty isn't used to rejection and is clearly going to be spurred on by it. Guys are guys—Up Here, Down There—makes no difference. I guess the easiest way to get rid of him would be to capitulate, tell him I love him, and watch him run a mile in the opposite direction. But my integrity (another repeat trait) wouldn't let me pull a stunt like that.

I gave the flowers to Gail.

yawning

NAME Trevor Scalliwag
CAUSE OF DEATH Scabies
SUBJECT OF UPGRADE Yawning
REASON FOR UPGRADE Anything would be an improvement.

UPGRADE SUGGESTION Yawning is unattractive. Could it be replaced with singing?

The Sleep department is notoriously hard to get hold of. By the time you've got through to them and they've gone through the backlog, it's normally the end of the day. And then you have to start the whole process again the following day. I did speak to someone at 4 p.m. who said to send an email with the suggested changes and that someone will take a look at it in a few days. Or weeks. He said to keep it brief.

TO: SLEEP DEPT
FROM: UPDATES TEAM
SUBJECT: Replacing yawning with "singing"—doable?
Please respond ASAP.

In the meantime, I am going to look into the repercussions.

Pros:
- If you had a good voice, this would be a great way to showcase your talent.
- Bedtime could be melodious.
- Yawning IS unattractive.

Cons:
- Lots of people have terrible voices.
- Bedtime could be a cacophonous mess.
- What if you were in the middle of a conversation? A yawn can be stifled. Can a song?
- Imagine the late train home. Unbearable.

BUTTOCKS

NAME Wendy Peng
CAUSE OF DEATH Rap battle
SUBJECT OF UPGRADE Buttocks
REASON FOR UPGRADE They don't do much.

UPGRADE SUGGESTION Buttocks are underutilized. They should clap, or pick things up, or be used to store magazines.

Wendy has managed to make three different suggestions on one feedback form, showing an admirable efficiency. If I'm ever allowed to hire an assistant, I will look her up.

Here goes.

1. Buttocks should clap: As long as you're not sitting down, and if you have your hands full, this could possibly be useful. At a gig, holding a couple of drinks? Do you ever need to clap while skiing?

2. Buttocks should pick things up: Again, only if your hands were full. You would have to squat down pretty low to pick something up with your buttocks, and I can't see it being used very often. I don't think you need to pick things up while skiing either. Perhaps we should consider lowering them on the body, say down to the calf?

3. Buttocks should be used to store magazines: That's more like it. Let's imagine the standard household size (two adults, two children). A quick calculation says each pair of buttocks could hold three standard magazines (not *Vogue*), meaning an average family would have mobile buttock storage for a year's worth of one monthly magazine. If you subscribe to more magazines, simply have more children. Brilliant.

GOLF

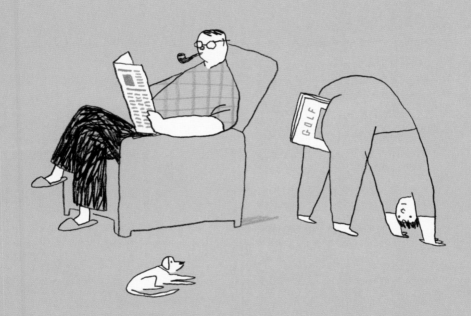

Up Here's social media presence was officially launched today. We have one platform that everyone uses called UHgram. Our feed racked up twenty-nine followers by the end of the day (mostly just cynical interns who wanted to see how many cat pics Fran would post). Still, The Boss is committed to modernizing, so here we are. Today's post was just the new logo. I'm sure Fran knows what she's doing.

Sleeping

NAME Hercule Zeitgeist
CAUSE OF DEATH Plunge pool
SUBJECT OF UPGRADE Sleeping
REASON FOR UPGRADE Save space

UPGRADE SUGGESTION Humans should sleep standing up, like horses. That would free up bedrooms to be used as home gyms, dance studios, or walk-in wardrobes.

Leaving aside the fact that bedrooms aren't only used for sleeping (ahem, Hercule), this is an interesting one. Humans would still need somewhere to sleep, regardless of their sleeping position. You can't have people standing asleep on the street; they could get mugged. If you are in your own home, fair enough, but if you live with someone, they won't want to have to creep around you while they're having a dinner party.

Think of the holidays when Grandpa John falls asleep, full of turkey. He'd be standing alongside the dinner table swaying back and forth. But if he's snoring, and therefore creating electricity, we could charge our phones. Maybe there's something to this.

Conclusion: You're still going to need a "sleep room." And beds are great! What about those lazy Sunday mornings, when you get the papers and the dog and stay in bed until noon? What about sleepovers with your girlfriends? What about waking up from a nightmare and getting into bed with your parents? Tent design? None of this works if you're just standing in the corner of a room with your eyes closed. No, no, no.

In fact, I'm going to turn this around and start a petition to get horses to sleep lying down. In beds. It's only fair.

The UHgram account posted a proper post today: "It's all you can eat pasta day at the cafeteria! Tell us your favorite pasta dish with the hashtag #I♥MYNOODLE!" There were a lot of responses. My favorite: "I like puttanesca because it reminds me of your mom."

Voice

NAME Natalia Sharypova
CAUSE OF DEATH Greased lightning
SUBJECT OF UPGRADE Voice
REASON FOR UPGRADE Fairness

UPGRADE SUGGESTION Your voice should run out if you speak for too long.

This has come up a few times already. The last time was at a meeting, when The Boss was giving His annual review. (I usually bring snacks to sustain myself.) Someone else suggested it at the Xmas party, when The Boss was telling us about His elaborate plans for next year. And it was on a note Jonty passed me at our last Intern Motivation Session, which The Boss likes to conduct once a month.

We'd need to allow for a time limit—say, half an hour? Maybe a soft "ting" sound when the speaker reaches the cut-off point, and then silence. Ah, the silence.

I have a feeling this will be a unanimous yes. Although The Boss might have something (lengthy) to say about it.

Flesh Confetti

NAME Bippi MacBeth
CAUSE OF DEATH Chocolate martinis
SUBJECT OF UPGRADE Flesh confetti
REASON FOR UPGRADE Recycling

UPGRADE SUGGESTION The bits that come out of people's bodies when they get a piercing should be used as flesh confetti at weddings. Or dog food.

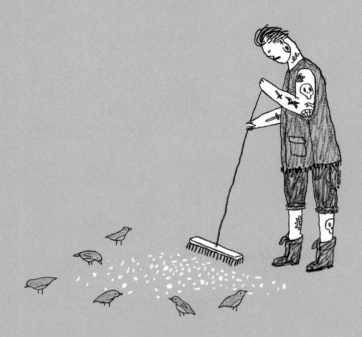

Currently, the bits that come out of people's bodies when they get a piercing are eaten by a species of bird. They hang around outside piercing salons, waiting for someone to sweep the floor, and then they swoop. David Attenborough has yet to notice, which is why the rest of Down There hasn't heard about them.

We could give them something else to eat. Off the top of my head . . . nail clippings? Hanging around menacingly outside nail bars isn't that different to hanging around menacingly outside piercing salons.

I put in a request to have an alternative menu drawn up for the birds, but then I got a call from an unknown number, advising me that "no one needs flesh confetti, OK? Leave our food alone." Then the line went dead.

I think The Boss is getting rid of weddings soon anyway, so let's just leave this as it is.

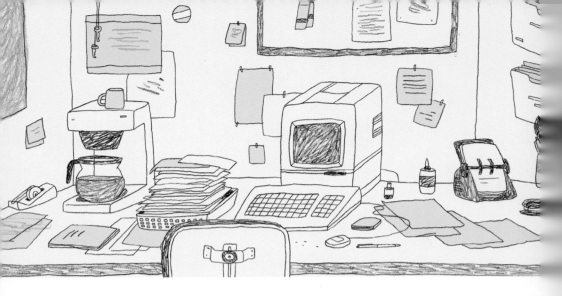

TIDYING UP THE TOLLBOOTH

Tom arranged for us to clean the tollbooth on Sunday. We usually aren't allowed to work on weekends, or holidays, but you can ask for a pass if there is a good enough reason. There was: the tollbooth was a mess. On Friday I discovered a nest of baby pigeons in an old T-shirt that had been shoved in the corner of the room. Gail found a moldy sandwich in her Cheery Greetings Suggestions Folder, and Tom drank a few gulps of something that most definitely wasn't coffee (unless coffee has bits of wax floating in it) in a cup that had been left on his desk. "Enough is enough," he spluttered, after he'd rinsed his mouth out with one of Gail's emergency diet sodas.

I wasn't really looking forward to it—my weekend plan was to hand-wash my collection of Icelandic fishermen's sweaters—but I didn't want to leave it up to Tom and Gail in case they accidentally threw away my files. They are often a bit slapdash with my paperwork. Plus, I believe in supporting my teammates, and we're so much closer since the party.

I turned up at 10 a.m. to find Tom in a pair of overalls with a baseball cap, dragging his desk onto the lawn outside the tollbooth. I put my bag down and gave him a hand. "Thought you were never going to turn up," he said, but kindly (Tom is always kind). He handed me overalls and a cap, just as Gail turned up in a hazmat suit with those white rubber boots you see on those crime documentaries she's always watching. She always goes one step further than everyone else.

Tom chose a "golden oldies" radio station as he said you can't beat a good sing-along when doing this kind of work. Then we started dragging everything outside and putting it into piles. Pretty soon we had a heap of broken electronic devices—printers, an old coffee machine, a mini-disc player—all that went to recycling. There was a mountain of paperwork to be sorted, but Gail started going through it, putting things into piles, and then gave up and put the whole lot in the "To Shred" sack. "What the heck, everyone's here who should be," she said, "and if they're not we'll find out about it soon enough."

We shredded bags of leaflets, ticket stubs, and receipts. There was a first-aid kit with all the Band-Aids missing; a Flemish–French dictionary; a box of those envelopes with windows that no one uses anymore; a dead spider plant (although what isn't dead, Up Here?); Gail's motivational plaques: "Die, Laugh, Love." Everything went into the trash.

Tom and I painted the walls white while singing along to a Doris Day medley, and Gail found an old gingham tablecloth and made some little curtains for both the hatches (Check-In and Out). I rescued a filing cabinet that has a lock on it (that actually works!), made labels for the drawers, and put all my important files in it.

We went for a late lunch to Tom's house, and when we made it back to the tollbooth, the paint had dried and everything looked pristine. We dragged the desks back inside, along with the filing cabinets and the one printer that actually worked. We arranged some trinkets on the shelf above my desk, and Gail put a bunch of daffodils in the vase. And I made a note to pick up a new tea kettle from Supplies. It was a surprisingly lovely day.

Speech Recall

NAME Bjorn Wag
CAUSE OF DEATH Diamonds on the soles of his shoes
SUBJECT OF UPGRADE Words
REASON FOR UPGRADE Embarrassment

UPGRADE SUGGESTION A "speech recall" function for when you say something in mixed company and no one hears you, and your words just hang there, and you wish you were dead.

Some interns were chatting in the cafeteria the other day about their favorite lives. Everyone was adding their two cents: "Venetian gondolier," "Samoan princess," "Medieval dentist" (that was Eric—I'm staying well away from him), and I joined in with "Ashanti warrior!!!!," but no one acknowledged me, and the conversation changed to something about custard and I KNOW I blushed.

I've made some calls. The Speech Team can insert a Recall button in the roof of your mouth, which you can press with your tongue if you regret saying something within three seconds of saying it (any longer and the words will have embedded into the brains of anyone nearby, and then they're impossible to remove).

The only drawback is that the words have to reenter the mouth and go back down the esophagus, and that can cause a sensation similar to acid reflux. You also have to keep your mouth open for the re-entry process, or the words will repeatedly bang against the lips and teeth and

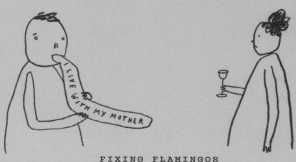

FIXING FLAMINGOS

can cause bruising and possible dental issues (don't tell Eric). There is also the possibility that the words could emerge a bit later from the other end, as flatulence, but "may not be as offensive as when they were originally spoken." (I beg to differ.) I'm trying to imagine what it would be like if my nether regions whispered "Ashanti warrior" later while I was back in the office with Gail. I'm pretty sure it would have been OK, as she has the radio on pretty loud most days.

I've been advised to conduct an informal poll, so I'll ask the next twenty people I speak to what they think. We are a democracy, after all.

COMPLIMENTS

NAME Babka Szabova
CAUSE OF DEATH Shark attack
SUBJECT OF UPGRADE Compliments
REASON FOR UPGRADE Bullshit

UPGRADE SUGGESTION A limit on compliments. They are so tedious, and no one ever means them. How about you can give four in a row, and the next one has to be honest. Enough with this bullshit.

We tried this out in the office. This is how it went:

Me to Gail:
1. Your hair looks great today.
2. I like your glasses.
3. Blue eyeshadow is so underrated.
4. You can never use too much perfume.
5. That mole looks like a fly died on your face.

She looked really hurt, and then took a deep breath.

Gail to Me:
1. Yellow is such a cheerful color on the young.
2. I love the way you mix all those fabrics so creatively.
3. I would totally wear lederhosen, too, if I had your figure.
4. The cape really shows off your ankles.
5. Your eyes are too close together.

When Tom came back from his toilet break, he found us both crying.

He took charge (it was very masterful) and said that this one is a terrible idea, and it's going straight into the shredder, and that neither of us meant it, and he loves moles, and you can do amazing things with eyeliner these days. Which was wise of him, because his shirt is too tight, his hair needs cutting, and he's spilled some egg yolk on his jeans, but neither of us is going to tell him that.

The UHG (as we are now calling the UHgram) has been quiet for a while, but today there was a photo of The Boss at His desk with a rigid smile on His face. The comment below it said, "Thank you everyone for your dedication to making this the BEST afterlife option available!" The truth is, even if we did nothing, we'd still be better than the alternative—unless you enjoy being torn limb-from-limb by rabid beasts, or dining with conspiracy theorists for all eternity.

Dating

NAME Vladimir Popov
CAUSE OF DEATH Scurvy
SUBJECT OF UPGRADE Dating
REASON FOR UPGRADE Honesty

UPGRADE SUGGESTION Dates should never take place in bars or restaurants in your best clothes with good lighting. They must be set in your kitchen in dirty loungewear so you can imagine being married to that person. Ideally you should factor in an argument about milk.

The Boss programmed romance Himself. All chat-up lines are His—even the vulgar ones. He spends an hour or so once a week adding new ones (a sixteen-year-old today wouldn't get very far using a medieval line comparing his beloved to his prize sheep, for example).

Dating is the human equivalent of arranging your tail feathers to look like a giant face and dancing back and forth in a jungle clearing. (He really wanted humans to be able to do that but arranging your buttocks to look like a giant face, although doable, doesn't have the desired effect.)

He isn't going to approve this one, as He's really proud of mating rituals for all species. Everyone—from humans to birds to slugs—needs to pretend they're someone better than they really are when performing their mating ritual. Vladimir is basically saying "be yourself" in this suggestion. Which is terrible, terrible advice.

Today's UHG question of the day: "Who were you? Send us a photo of your #lastlife." It was quiet for a bit and then the responses started to trickle in—one of the Hair guys used to be in the Beatles, and my favorite cafeteria server invented fish sticks. Closer to home, we discovered Tom was a chorus girl in the 1930s, which made Gail and me giggle so hard I had to run out to the bathroom and wash my face in cold water. The photo was a bit grainy, but you could tell he had great legs.

WEDDING GUESTS

NAME Tim Flammable
CAUSE OF DEATH Stampede
SUBJECT OF UPGRADE Weddings
REASON FOR UPGRADE Just to be sure

UPGRADE SUGGESTION Wedding guests should be limited
to all the people the couple has slept with. The priest
should also be someone they've slept with. Then the couple
walk down the aisle scrutinizing all their past partners
and they decide when they reach the altar if they still
want to get married.

In the name of research, I just tried imagining this with my last life. I definitely wouldn't have married my husband if I'd had to walk down the aisle past Blake, who I met at twenty-three. (The train we were both traveling on was stranded in a blizzard for twelve hours. Sigh.)

Or Jeff, come to think of it. Or Franco, or Takeshi, or Nick, or Phil, or Samson, or Julie, or Leon, or Katie, or Don. And definitely not Reverend Shaw, Hopalong Sally, or the Admiral.

This makes me uncomfortable.

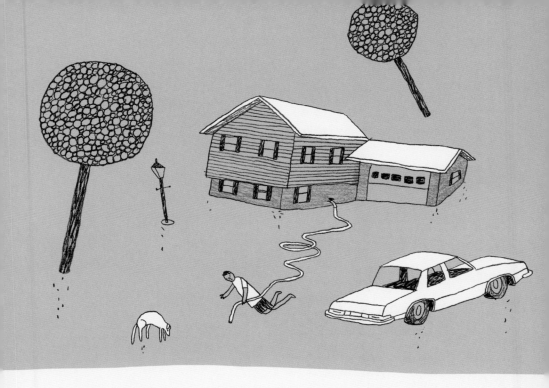

Gravity

NAME Xavier Doodle

CAUSE OF DEATH Stuffed crust

SUBJECT OF UPGRADE Gravity

REASON FOR UPGRADE Deserves a break

UPGRADE SUGGESTION Gravity takes a day off once in a while—it must be exhausting pulling everything down all the time without a break. Do you not have employment laws Up Here?

I took this over to HR and showed it to Cheech, one of the interns. He said they were having a big meeting about squirrels (again?) but that he would take this in as soon as they were done and get back to me.

Result: HR is now in talks with Gravity about taking some time off. Cheech was listening in and he told me all about it. They suggested a day off per week, but that would be too disruptive. So they are looking to go with one second per hour, for the rest of eternity. Gravity can loosen the grip for a second, take a brief rest, and then pull it all back. It will work better than taking a bigger chunk of time off (and risking all matter floating off into space).

Cheech said he hopes it feels like when you drive over a little humped bridge, and your tummy goes funny. It's something to look forward to in my next life, anyway.

Dog Walks

NAME Septimus Fledermaus
CAUSE OF DEATH Chowder
SUBJECT OF UPGRADE Dogs
REASON FOR UPGRADE More power to 'em.

UPGRADE SUGGESTION If you're on a dog walk and you bump into someone you know, you are only allowed to talk if the dog says it's OK.

This is a request for the redistribution of power from humans to dogs, and to be honest, I've heard a lot of talk about this around here. Tom even said that The Boss is thinking about handing the whole thing over to dogs and putting them in charge. Tom said to send this one straight upstairs and not get involved, as it's a sensitive issue.

Today's UHG post: "Find your friends! If there's someone you have lost touch with since arriving Up Here, post their name and a short description with the hashtag #whereareyou." Cue lots of responses, such as "I'm looking for Francis who ran a laundromat in Boca Raton around 1954.

You still owe me $56. #whereareyou." And "Anyone know what happened to my father? He died in Cornwall in 1776. I would really like to know whether he fell off a cliff or was eaten by the Beast of the Moor. #whereareyou."

Whiskers

NAME Wanda Halibut
CAUSE OF DEATH Stage fright
SUBJECT OF UPGRADE Whiskers
REASON FOR UPGRADE Security

UPGRADE SUGGESTION Whiskers should sound like Klaxons when they brush past something.

I was feeling extra-efficient this morning, so I sent this over to Felines first thing with a request for a job spec. I received their response within two hours:

SPEC: Adding Klaxon to whiskers.
Sound design: 6.3 hours
Rewiring: 10.25 hours
Testing: 320 hours
Installation: 7.6 hours
Drawbacks: Loss of stealth mode; embarrassment; impaired hunting; embarrassment; cleaning will be a disaster; embarrassment
Benefits: None

PS: This will only end badly for you.

I don't think we need to take this any further.

Fish

NAME Hephzibah Winkleman-Cherry
CAUSE OF DEATH Poké bowl
SUBJECT OF UPGRADE Fish
REASON FOR UPGRADE Want to get to know them better.

UPGRADE SUGGESTION Fish should learn sign language or mime, so we can talk to them while they're in the fish tank.

Soon there won't be any fish tanks, under The Boss's new rules, but this still applies to the ocean, river, or ornamental pond.

Everyone knows mime is useless, and only works if you're pretending to go downstairs behind a couch, or to be trapped behind an invisible wall. Fish don't need to do either of those things. So let's focus on sign language.

Without even looking at a fish today I can safely say their fins currently aren't long enough for sign language. They will have to be lengthened, and we will need hands for the more detailed words.

Questions for Fish Department:

1. Can we enlarge fins across the species?
2. Are there any negative impacts from fish having long "arms" instead of fins?
3. Will they use this to communicate between themselves?
4. Actually, how do fish talk to each other now?
5. Do fish currently want to be able to talk to humans? There's no point in facilitating communication if they're not interested.

They Replied:

1. Yes, we can do a simple percentage growth with hand addition across all fish—will take about eight hours.

you can check
out anytime
you like, but
you can
never leave

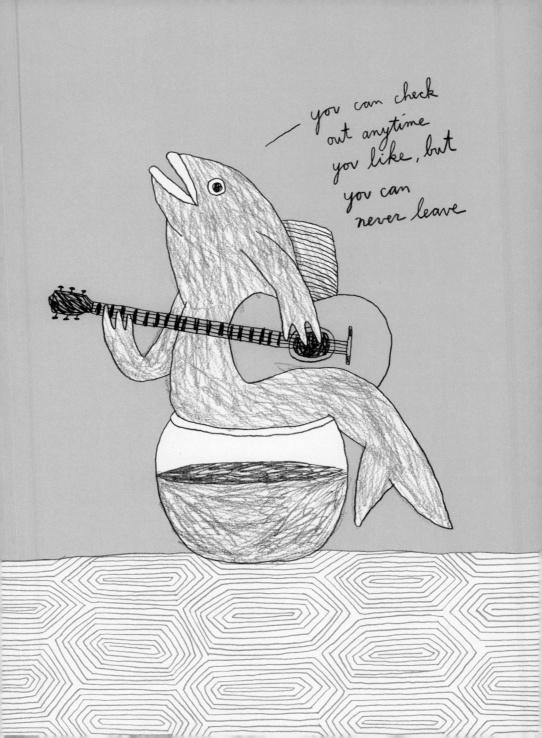

2. The only thing that has stopped fish from learning guitar is that their fins haven't been long enough. Fish are obsessed with guitars. We could be looking at billions of fish, all playing guitar, across all oceans, rivers, and garden ponds.
3. If they're playing guitar all the time, no.
4. CLASSIFIED.
5. Yes, about guitars.

Lightning

NAME Clay Dawood
CAUSE OF DEATH Spelunking
SUBJECT OF UPGRADE Lightning
REASON FOR UPGRADE Fun?

UPGRADE SUGGESTION When there is a lightning flash, you can see through everyone's clothes, so you can see what they look like naked for a second.

I don't like this, because Clay just sounds like a creep. But let's unpack this to humor him.

Query: Lightning flashes and people look naked.
Is this doable? Yes.
Should it be done? No.

Looks like we have an answer, Clay. Better luck next time!

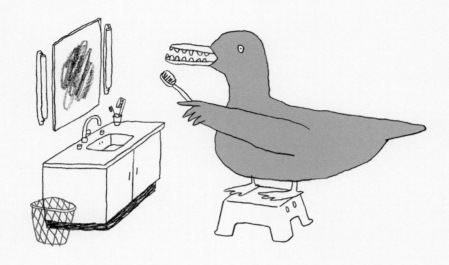

Ducks

NAME Battenburg De Silva

CAUSE OF DEATH Donut allergy

SUBJECT OF UPGRADE Ducks

REASON FOR UPGRADE Diet variety

UPGRADE SUGGESTION Ducks should have big teeth. They'd be able to eat more than bread if they could actually chew properly.

I sent a request to Birds for more information. They sent one of their interns to meet with me. (I can't work out if that's insulting or not.) Anyway, Trudy is cool—we met in the cafeteria to go over what she had dug out for me.

Ducks used to have sizeable teeth, and ate a range of foods that required chewing, including carrots, calamari, and beef jerky. The problem was they were unable to brush them, as you can't hold a toothbrush with a wing.

Something had to change, because a flock of ducks with toothaches is particularly disruptive to the surrounding ecology. The original designers were asked to come up with an answer—it came down to whether to revise the wing to accommodate a hand, or get rid of the teeth altogether and limit their food consumption to softer items.

Ducks were asked what they would prefer. Nearly all of them were all for adding the hand (and therefore, the toothbrush), until the newly appointed Duck Dentist said they really should include flossing for it to be a complete dental hygiene regime. And that was the last straw—the ducks decided unanimously that life was too short for that kind of thing, so they got rid of teeth altogether.

Trudy said they are planning to ask the ducks again, as they like to check in every few generations. Dental hygiene has moved on since it was last broached, with toothbrushes going electric, for example, but lack of charging facilities in lakes mean they are out of reach for most ducks.

WELL-BEING

Today's morning UHG post got everyone talking. "It's well-being day! We've sent some massage angels out to offer each of you a treatment at your desk! There will also be mini-muffins!"

Just before lunchtime, a young man dressed in white appeared at the door of the tollbooth. (I'm always wary of people who wear all white. I feel like they're compensating for something.) However, Milan the

Massage Guy (according to his business card) seems sweet enough. "Head and shoulder massage, courtesy of The Boss," he said. "Who's first?"

Gail squeaked (I've never heard her do that before) and dragged him over to her side of the tollbooth. Within seconds she was listing to one side and had spilled a cup of tea all over her desk. When it was over, she declared she was going home to sort her hair out. "I'm the first person these poor souls see when they get Up Here, and they're not expecting Alice Cooper."

Tom said I could go next, because he would, wouldn't he? It was divine—I hadn't realized how tense I was. Of course, it was terrible for productivity, as I was unable to think about leg lengths or moveable hair for hours afterwards. I pretended to do research for the rest of the afternoon by flicking through an old issue of *National Geographic*.

Tom moaned and sighed rather a lot during his treatment. I turned the radio up to drown him out, which thankfully also drowned out three phone calls from Jonty. However, it meant I didn't hear the knock of the mini-muffins delivery guy, which will have to count as collateral damage.

Cold Sweat

NAME Jemima Twinge
CAUSE OF DEATH Spatula rage
SUBJECT OF UPGRADE Sweat
REASON FOR UPGRADE It doesn't work.

UPGRADE SUGGESTION I don't think sweat is cold enough to cool you down. It should be icy. Surely that would work better?

I put in a request with the Body Temperature department and they've given us two options:

1. A refrigeration "layer" under the epidermis that freezes sweat as it emerges from the sweat glands. This will be powered by a tiny fridge motor located in the base of the skull and comes with a handy light that switches on when you raise your arms. This is the most effective option, but it will be very expensive for obvious reasons (they maxed out on the skin budget already, giving us so many—in my opinion unnecessary—layers).
2. A refrigeration unit located on the top of the head. All sweat would be rerouted to the crown, cooled, and then poured from the top of the head down the body. This is by far the cheapest but causes a number of problems. The addition of a small box on the top of the head would impact hat design, hair design, and synchronized diving. And having the sweat streaming down the body from the top of the head could cause temporary blindness, not to mention the possibility of drowning.

One point: The mechanism will have to be disabled for people who live in Scandinavia, for example, but activated when they go on holiday to the Mediterranean.

I've included both options in my report for upstairs, and I'm really hoping He's not going to go for either of them.

Animal Ears

NAME Felicity Cowface
CAUSE OF DEATH Fashion
SUBJECT OF UPGRADE Cats and dogs
REASON FOR UPGRADE It would look snazzy.

UPGRADE SUGGESTION Cats and dogs would look better with human ears, and then they could wear earrings.

I called a meeting with someone from Felines, someone from Canines, and someone from Ears. There was a lot of shouting, but eventually I was able to take control of the room (after picking up the snack items that were thrown). They've all agreed to send over new designs and we are meeting again in a couple of weeks.

I'm quite pleased with my diplomacy skills today, as they are notoriously difficult departments to deal with. And we are potentially making quite big changes to their designs. I am looking forward to seeing what they come up with, but more than that, I am excited about how much I have grown in my ability to command respect, despite only being a few weeks into this position. I just hope people have started to notice.

ReTRacTable Necks

NAME Bongs Oumarou
CAUSE OF DEATH Cage fighting
SUBJECT OF UPGRADE Necks
REASON FOR UPGRADE Travel comfort

UPGRADE SUGGESTION Let's have retractable necks for better sleeping on planes.

The Boss can be very stubborn at times (sometimes? All the time) and this one is going to be a no-no. He recently refused the request for humans to be able to sleep standing up. He says that if you can't work out how to get yourself to bed when you're tired, you don't deserve a good night's sleep. I've seen petitions asking for, at the very least, a rigid neck, but He's ignored all of them.

He obviously has never had to fly on a low-budget airline at 1 a.m. to a low-budget airport fifty miles away from the actual city you plan to have your low-budget mini-break in. It's clearly one rule for the Ultimate Creator of the Universe, and one for the rest of us.

I will approve this just to see what happens when it goes upstairs for Phase 2, but only because I'm in that kind of mood today.

Bladders

NAME Roisin Cake
CAUSE OF DEATH Musical theater
SUBJECT OF UPGRADE Urinary system
REASON FOR UPGRADE Time management

UPGRADE SUGGESTION Bladders need to be much, much bigger. They can't employ the current "one [drink] in, one [drink] out" system forever. It's so annoying having to find a toilet on a night out and miss all the good conversation. If we had bigger bladders, you could just store all the beer you drink at a festival, for example, and then do one massive wee when you get home. Anything to avoid the hunt for a vacant, slightly less filthy Porta Potty at 4 a.m.

In my last life I had meant to go to Woodstock, but I took a wrong turn and ended up in Scranton. It turns out that Scranton has a good number of very clean public conveniences, which is the main (OK, only) memory I have of that weekend. They say if you can remember Woodstock, you weren't really there, while I say there's also a chance you turned off the highway too soon in your camper van.

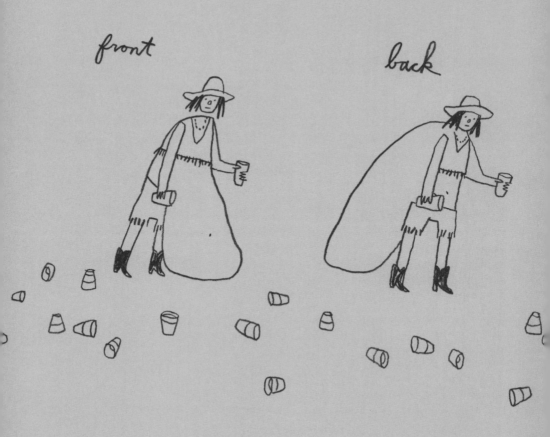

front

back

So yes, I am fully behind this one. We need to look into where the extra-large bladder would be stored. If the average human produces three pints of urine on a normal day, we will need to double that if they are drinking beer at a festival. Actually, let's triple it to be safe. So we need to be able to hold nine pints of urine in our extended bladder.

I have requested a couple of sketches of what this would look like—one on the back and one where the bladder currently lives.

Update: the sketches came back. The last day of the festival now looks either like a day at a camel race, or chaos at a maternity ward.

Ear Wicks

NAME Xenia Belafonte
CAUSE OF DEATH Balloons
SUBJECT OF UPGRADE Ears
REASON FOR UPGRADE Usefulness

UPGRADE SUGGESTION If we could grow ear wicks to go with ear wax, we'd always have candles within reach—useful in a blackout.

Everyone I've mentioned this to has said the same thing—brilliant idea, but also potentially quite dangerous, so must be handled with care.

I think this needs one of my lists:

Pros:
- Great in a blackout—no need to panic if there is an electricity outage
- Camping—need the bathroom after dark? Simply light your ear wicks and head out, keeping your hands free
- Would add an extra romantic element to dinner time, if both parties had their ear candles lit

Cons:
- You could set your hair on fire
- You could set your surroundings on fire
- You could set other people on fire

I called Ears again. They will look into whether growing a wick inside the ear would affect hearing and get back to me. A lot of this job is waiting to hear from people. I'm so glad I have an efficient spreadsheet system, or I could get really confused. Side note: Ears are a fun bunch. When I called them out of hours I got their voicemail. It was just a recording of someone saying, "What? WHAT? I'm sorry . . . what? BEEP."

Small Hands

NAME Ben Cormorant
CAUSE OF DEATH Schadenfreude
SUBJECT OF UPGRADE Hand size
REASON FOR UPGRADE Weight management

UPGRADE SUGGESTION Hands should be smaller. Like when you use a side plate at the breakfast buffet when you're on holiday to ensure you don't overeat.

I have enlisted the help of Dede, a toddler I met at lunch. She has tiny hands because she's a toddler, but also has the Wisdom of All Eternity (as we all do Up Here, which I know can come as a surprise). I've been giving Dede a variety of tasks.

Tasks that were harder with small hands: cleaning, kneading bread, construction, farming, eating burgers, playing piano/trombone/cello.

Tasks that were easier with small hands: crochet, macrame, gardening, surgery, eating sushi, playing the lute, and grabbing coins stuck beneath a car seat.

This may not be a problem, because we have probably built all the buildings we need Down There, lots of people have given up bread these days, and no one listens to the trombone. On the plus side, who doesn't love sushi and gardening, and a bit of amateur surgery on the weekends?

MEAT PRODUCTION

NAME Jimmy Pinstripe

CAUSE OF DEATH Tarot reading

SUBJECT OF UPGRADE Snacks

REASON FOR UPGRADE I can't eat tofu.

UPGRADE SUGGESTION Meat's kinda gross, but it tastes so good. Is there any way it could be kinder?

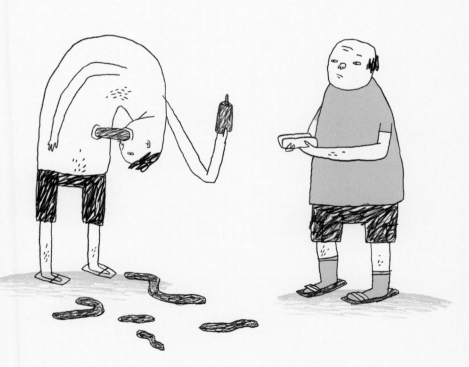

I know that people have been curious about the ethics of meat production for a while, and it's actually on the list that The Boss is working on right now. He never meant for us to eat each other, you know. Pigs were supposed to be celebrated for their great sense of humor. Cows give brilliant advice. Chickens are accomplished acupuncturists.

One of the things He is looking at is "self-generated meat." Basically, if you want to eat meat, you make it yourself. Someone was telling me yesterday in the cafeteria that they are working on meat that you manifest by asking for it. It's basically the law of attraction, but for bacon. They're thinking of the belly button as the exit point of the meat product; it's not like it's used for anything post-birth. Well, apart from keeping fluff, and that turned out to be less useful than He thought it would be.

Red Hair

NAME Jan Pigeon
CAUSE OF DEATH Vanity
SUBJECT OF UPGRADE Hair
REASON FOR UPGRADE More flattering

UPGRADE SUGGESTION Hair should turn red as you age, not gray. It's a much warmer color, and more flattering on the older person.

The Hair guys say it's easy to change the aging palette from "grays" to "reds" in the genome. They also said there is a lot of red dye left over since the number of natural redheads is falling, so this one is easy.

I'm just glad they were reasonably polite when I called them. I'm beginning to get a little hurt by the audible sighs when I make a phone call these days.

It looks like Fran is doing a pretty good job on the UHG stats. Apparently Up Here's account is up 4 million followers to 4,000,029 in just a couple of weeks. The Boss is really pleased and said if she carries on like this, He might consider sending her on a social media strategy course. Word is she was pretty insulted by this, which might explain why #TheBossfashionfails was trending for most of the afternoon.

Baby Beards

NAME Bill Billabong
CAUSE OF DEATH Skinny jeans
SUBJECT OF UPGRADE Baby facial hair
REASON FOR UPGRADE Useful knowledge

UPGRADE SUGGESTION Babies should be born with full beards just for the first day, so when they get older they will know if they should grow one or not.

I don't want to have to call the Hair guys again.

One Meal

NAME Dan Plank

CAUSE OF DEATH Burpees

SUBJECT OF UPGRADE One meal a year

REASON FOR UPGRADE Time-saving

UPGRADE SUGGESTION You should have an option to eat all your food for a year in one sitting and then not eat again until you've used up all the calories. This would be useful for fitness guys, intermittent fasters, explorers, and people who row across the Atlantic.

I know fasting became a thing Down There recently—I read a few articles on the internet about it while in the last care home. All the successful tech guys were eating once every thirty-eight hours and waking up at 3 a.m. and running twenty miles before their vitamin IV, and it all seemed rather unnecessary. Surely eating and sleeping are the best things in life. (Idea: What about eating while sleeping—that would be awesome. Although potentially quite messy.)

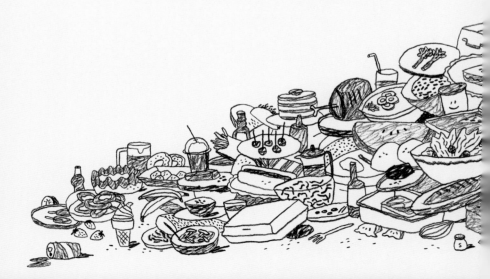

If we have managed to simplify the internal organs, this could be possible.

If the average human needs roughly 2000 calories per day, that equals 730,000 calories per year. That's around 3200 fried egg sandwiches in twenty-four hours, or two fried egg sandwiches per minute.

I get it, but the impacts will be seen across the board—dating, the hospitality sector, Christmas, Thanksgiving, Ramadan, going to the toilet (the day after Eating Day would not be pretty). Should we stagger Eating Days based on birth date? Should food amount be based on weight or height? What about snacking? This hurts my head. Maybe put this on hold until we hear the results of the internal organs review (and after I finish my bag of chips).

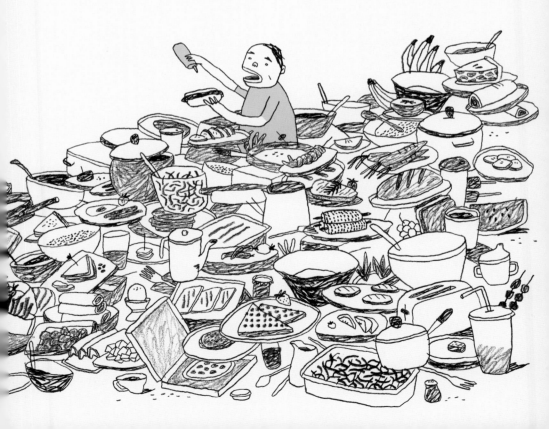

FLESH NECKTIES

NAME Lily Vanilli
CAUSE OF DEATH Buttercream
SUBJECT OF UPGRADE Neckties
REASON FOR UPGRADE Why not?

UPGRADE SUGGESTION Neckties should be made of flesh and be part of the body, like an extra limb.

I know The Boss well enough to know the first question He will ask: "Do we need an extra, necktie-shaped limb protruding from the neck?" So, let's try and answer that first.

The quick answer is probably not, but we should still look at what it could do:

- It could slap someone in the face if they got too close to you and you were holding shopping bags in both hands.
- It could touch up your makeup while you type (although without fingers it would only be good for the broader strokes).
- It could wave at people.
- It could stroke your baby's face while you breastfeed.
- It could probably do lots of things during the sex act (we don't need to go into details here).
- It would make boxing more interesting.

Extra limbs are easy to encode, but they do need to be justified. Also, what does this mean for necktie producers? And could people be born with the normal straightforward necktie limb, and the bow-tie limb, and the skinny piano tie limb? What about that weird one that cowboys have?

Farts

NAME Cornelius Sandwich
CAUSE OF DEATH Ziplining
SUBJECT OF UPGRADE Farts
REASON FOR UPGRADE Isn't it obvious?

UPGRADE SUGGESTION When you fart, you get a "fartune cookie" that tells you your future.

This is a joke, really—Cornelius is being silly, because of the pun. Also, it only really works in English (as far as I know; I only speak 4,823 languages, and it doesn't work in any of those).

However, it's actually a really good idea.

Obviously, we wouldn't want to tell anyone their real fortunes, because that's classified. But there's nothing wrong with a little uplifting message every once in a while.

However, I'm not happy with anything "tangible" coming from the rectal area, if you know what I mean. No one wants to be pulling little rice paper messages out of their buttholes, however cheery the message.

So, I would modify this to an "audible" fartune, that replaces the unpleasant (although very amusing) sound of a fart.

Update: Turns out this will be pretty easy. We've got Janice, an intern over in Speech, recording an extensive list of uplifting messages in all possible languages. It should take her a day or two. This will replace the audio file currently used for fart noises. Apparently, The Boss was looking into changing this but hadn't gotten round to it (story of His life, it seems). So we can try this out for a few generations and see how it goes. Whether it cheers people up more than a loud unexpected bum-raspberry, however, is yet to be seen.

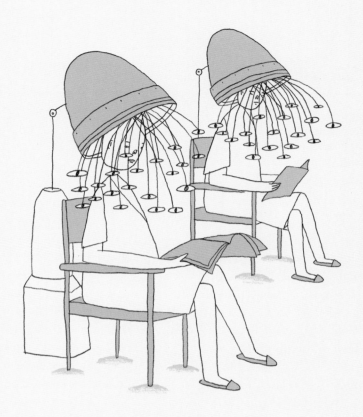

HAIR EYES

NAME Zsa-Zsa Goodenough

CAUSE OF DEATH Sinking

SUBJECT OF UPGRADE Hair

REASON FOR UPGRADE 360-degree vision

UPGRADE SUGGESTION Each hair should have an eyeball at the end.

FIXING FLAMINGOS

Warning: We have other hair updates pending. We can't choose all of them. (And I really, REALLY don't want to have to call Hair again.)

Let's look at this first (with just my two eyeballs). We have about 100,000 hairs on our heads. If we had 100,002 eyeballs, life would be unbearable, surely? We'd see people pulling faces behind our backs. We'd see people stealing chocolate bars in the supermarket. We'd be on edge all the time.

No. Plus it would look awful; it would ruin hairstyles; and hairdressers would be traumatized. I am throwing this in the trash.

Bottoms/Buttocks/Bums

NAME Jilly Bibbles
CAUSE OF DEATH MMA fight
SUBJECT OF UPGRADE Bottoms/buttocks/bums
REASON FOR UPGRADE Financial

UPGRADE SUGGESTION Bottoms should really be at the bottom of the body, and replace legs and feet, saving money on trousers and shoes. Also ballet would be more interesting.

```
EVALUATING CRITERIA
Definition of command ⊠BOTTOM⊠ in Webster's
Dictionary:
The underside of something
Buttocks, rump
CONCLUSION
BOTTOM = BUTTOCKS/UNDERSIDE OF SOMETHING
MOTION CONFIRMED AND APPROVED
```

Right. Let me explain what just happened.

Gary, a creep from the IT department (OK, he may not be a creep, but he does wear a long leather coat, which would result in immediate termination if I was in charge) had replaced a toner cartridge in our booth last week. He saw the feedback forms piling up on my desk and decided I was struggling. So, he had the "brilliant idea" (his words, not mine) to approach The Boss about making my job automated.

OK, things ARE busy, but I've clearly got it under control. But Gary thinks a machine would save everyone time and improve productivity. (I hate that word; it's always used by people with dubious priorities and five-year plans.) Whatever, Gary.

The result? When I turned up for work this morning, there it was—a cream-colored box installed by Gail's Check-In window, whirring away. There was a label taped to the front in all caps: A B B Y 3 0 0 0. The spacing between the letters was almost as annoying as the pink label. Pink! How patronizing. Gary is a dick.

The morning's new arrivals were already lined up at Gail's window busily filling in the redesigned feedback forms, now called Improvement Proposal Forms (IPFs). Then they moved off to queue in another line to insert the forms into ABBY 3000's IPF Entry Slot.

I sat at my desk watching this nightmare unfold while I picked at a piece of tape from the edge of my chair and contemplated how best to make an IT nerd (and his horrible coat) disappear.

As I suspected, things began to unravel quickly. First, ABBY 3000 didn't recognize the ink from the pens, so about two hundred entries were lost. When people in the queue were told they would have to fill out their IPFs again, I thought a riot was going to break out. There was some shouting, things got heated, and Gail had to hand out her emergency stash of crackers to keep the peace. When Gary finally arrived with the correct pens (declaring enthusiastically, "It's great, isn't it!?"), it was chaos.

The first IPF filled out with the right pen was inserted into the ABBY 3000. The machine made a clunking noise and eventually a receipt dropped out of another slot. I picked it up. "PROPOSAL 'BOTTOMS' CONFIRMED. TAKE THIS SLIP TO THE UPGRADE DEPARTMENT."

At that point Gail intercepted, grabbed the receipt out of my hand, and called The Boss's direct line. She did that angry shouting yet whispering thing she does when she's really angry. I could only make out a few words, but I'm sure I heard "ridiculous idea," "get rid of LEGS?," "worried about Your grasp on reality," and one that I can't bring myself to repeat.

Result: ABBY 3000 was declared "unable to comprehend the implications of improvement proposals" and has been recycled into a (really useful) snack machine. Gary has been sent back Down There (The Boss wants him working in a supermarket on minimum wage) and I'm being given a Minor Upgrades Team to help me out, along with a promotion. I'm no longer an intern! I can't say I'll miss the lunches.

The Boss called me to the large meeting room to apologize, which is pretty good of Him, considering how busy He is. He asked me if there was anything I wanted—a cafeteria voucher, or a new desk, maybe a plant? I waved away His offers. "No," I said, "I want You to hear me out." I pulled up a chair.

"I really care about my job, and if You don't mind me saying, that's why I was always going to be better than any so-called ABBY 3000."

Then I got a bit emotional. "This job requires care and understanding—especially of Down There," I told Him. "I loved all my lives. I love the trees and the mountains, the cities and the towns, the successes and the disappointments. I love running in the rain and lying in the sun." At this, The Boss nodded, and smiled wistfully, eyes closed. I continued (I was on a roll): "A machine could never wonder what it might feel like to stroke the soft fur of a massive bee, or what style sweater would look best on a midsize sheep, or how best to pick up an issue of *People* magazine using one's buttocks."

He was quiet for a while, nodding and stroking His beard, and then He smiled and said: "How about popping Down There and putting together a report on how the updates are going so far?" I said I would be delighted. I miss the old place.

So at the end of the week, I'll be heading Down There to review things. I don't have to start a new life—I'll just visit as a ghost, which works best for a short trip. Lots of floating about, which is really fun. The Boss made me promise there would be no rattling chains, disembodied voices, or haunting though. That's really frowned upon.

When I got back to my desk, Tom and Gail had bought me a cherry soda from the repurposed AbbySnack 3000 (great invention, Gary), and my phone was ringing. It was The Boss. "Abby? Don't go ruffling any feathers, especially pink ones!" and then He put the phone down, sniggering.

I really do despair.